LOVE YOU TO HEAVEN AND BACK

Love You to Heaven and Back

OVERCOMING GRIEF WITH PRAISE

Denelle Scanlan

Chris Scanlan

Denelle Scanlan

Published by Denelle Scanlan the Author, Lake Havasu City, Arizona

ISBN 9798218415532 (Paperback)
9798218415549 (EPUB)

First Printing, 2024

Dedicated

To Sammy, the baby who made me a mama and taught me about a much more profound love than I had known could exist with the exception of the ultimate love from Jesus.

To Micah who taught me to never give up, and that true joy can come even in the midst of grief.

To Hosanna who taught me that the Lord of Hope is still working His miracles today!

To Hezekiah who taught me the value of true strength from the Lord.

To my family and friends who have been on this journey with me, I am eternally grateful for your love.

To Nathan for printing my first manuscript, the dream team for editing with a fine-tooth comb, and my launch team for helping to get this book into the hands of those who could benefit greatly.

To all the parents who have had their babies born into Heaven, I pray this journey together helps your heart to heal.

Contents

Disclaimer

This book is presented solely for informational and personal purposes. Neither of the authors nor other contributors shall be held liable to any person or entity with respect to any incident or damage as indirect or direct result to the information within. This should not be used as a substitute for seeking the assistance of a mental health professional, doctor, and/or pastor. Furthermore, the views held by the authors and other contributors in this book vary based on experiences, education, and religious background. In fact, the authors are still working through some of their experiences themselves. Readers are urged to seek out the Truth for themselves.

Author's Note

This book may seem an odd contrast to my first, *Sex in Marriage: From a Four-Letter Word to a Holy Act.* However, it is very much a continuation of my previous writings. For those of you who have not read it, that book follows my personal journey to seek the Lord's healing in my heart in the area of sexual intimacy with my husband. You see, I grew up in the purity culture, embracing the idea that "sex is a sin." That's it. There was nothing else to follow that untrue statement, which proved to be a very difficult lie to overcome. By the end of my book, I still hadn't been completely healed, though I had made significant progress. I continued praying, asking other godly men and women their advice and prayers, and seeking the Lord's heart.

As you read this book, I have included journaling prompts and Bible verses similar to my previous publication. However, this journey is one that is undoubtedly even harder, and some readers might not be ready to read everything, or you might not agree with the things I have experienced or the perspective I hold. That's okay. Please use the prompts and our story to aid you in your own healing journey. Take your time. Give yourself grace. I warn you that beginning this journey will likely rip open old wounds or bring things to light that you have tried so hard to hide, but it's one worth taking. Healing is often painful, but if we are patient, and honest, it is possible.

In contrast to my previous publication, my husband, Chris has become a co-author. It is heavy on our hearts that his contributions help to aid daddies of babies in Heaven. There are many resources and groups out there for mothers, but few for fathers who are generally expected to support the mothers, swallow their own emotions, and move forward without mention of the pain in *their* hearts. My writings occur first, followed by Chris' reflections on those writings.

> "All praise to God, the Father of our Lord Jesus Christ. God is our merciful Father and the source of all comfort. He comforts us in all our troubles so that we can comfort others. When they are troubled, we will be able to give them the same comfort God has given us."
>
> (2 Corinthians 1:3-4 NLT)

Part I- Born to be a Mommy

1

Marisol

Ninety-nine, one hundred! Mom! Dad! I finally have one hundred dollars!" One excited little girl came sprinting out of her room, with pennies clanging everywhere in her Winnie the Pooh piggy bank. After about thirty minutes of counting to be sure, her parents confirmed that yes, she had indeed saved $100. The deal was, she saved enough money to buy the 2005 limited edition American Girl Doll, Marisol, while her parents agreed to pay for the shipping and handling. That girl was me. I had collected pennies for months so that I could purchase my own American Girl Doll. I wanted her so that my other one, Ashley, who had been a Christmas surprise years before, could have a friend with whom to play. When Marisol finally made her way home, I gingerly unwrapped the box, and cared for Marisol and Ashley as my own children. Even then, when I was merely in 5th grade, I dreamed of one day giving them to my own daughter. She would treasure them just as I had, and we would enjoy playing with them together.

2

Ashley

The summer of 2012 just before leaving for college, I had staffed for two-and-a-half weeks as a Mission Builder with Youth With a Mission (YWAM) in Mexico. It was my first time on my own in missions away from family and my church youth group. I faced a very trying time due to confusion on what exactly I was supposed to be doing, but when God gave me the opportunity to go on outreach with other teams, I joyfully went. I had trained with the outreach teams, but then one day, when it came to going, I was told that I needed to help with the hospitality. I was allowed to go on outreach with the teams only if my hospitality duties had been finished. This time, it was to an orphanage to share what we had been learning. Unlike the ones in the media that give orphanages a bad rap for pretending to be in need in order to receive more donations, *this* orphanage was beautiful; the workers truly cared for the kids, and the kids loved their staff. Many of the children were living there as their parents were fighting to become clean from substance abuse, or trying to make a better living so they could afford more. However, some were indeed orphans and were praying for adoption. Ashley was one of those beautiful little girls. I was barely an adult myself, having just graduated high school, and she was already eight years old, but there was something about Ashley that made my heart yearn to adopt her. We visited that orphanage a couple more times during my short stay. I started to look seriously into how to make it possible to adopt this sweet girl. I wanted to bring her to live with me as I went to university to help us both have a great life. Then, one day, the man who would be my future husband would fall in love with her too. Looking back, of course, I realize that I romanticized how life would be as a single mama to an adopted daughter from Mexico, but I still do remember her and think about her often. I pray she did find a forever family to give her the love I wanted to give. Ultimately, due to being a single American with very little money to my name, I obviously could not adopt her. However, when I recounted everything to my parents, neither was shocked. I was *born* to be a mama. I couldn't *wait* until I could adopt or have my own.

Your Turn: Did you want to be a parent? When you found out you were expecting, what are some things you dreamed of?

Part II-When God Said "No"

"Just as you cannot understand the path of the wind or the mystery of a tiny baby growing in its mother's womb, so you cannot understand the activity of God, who does all things."
(Ecclesiastes 11:5 NLT)

3

Sammy's Story

This story begins with the immense healing I had finally received after two years of marriage, though not yet complete. Chris, my incredibly patient and faithful husband and I started our life of living abroad as missionaries to a foreign country in the summer of 2018. For safety and security reasons of those with whom we ministered, I will name that first country, Las Montañas. While in Las Montañas, God gave Chris and I the opportunity to take a school called Word by Heart. This school is most accurately described as a school to teach believers how to dig deep into the Word of God, experience the stories, miracles, and teachings of Jesus for ourselves, and retell those stories as our own testimonies with firm conviction.

On Mondays during this school, the staff give teachings to enable students to see the stories taking place. These teachings include questions to aid in imagining some of the other details of the story that are left out, history lessons, and any other background that would bring clarity to the stories. One particular Monday, the topic of oneness in marriage arose, and our teacher discussed a study that was conducted, which essentially showed that when a husband and wife are intimate, parts of their DNA mix with their partners'. While the results of this study of microchimerism are controversial at best, and may or may not be true, this statement served to get me thinking, nonetheless. My husband and I had not had the opportunity to make this happen. We had been intimate, of course, but not to the fullness the Lord had intended. So, I began praying. By this time, we had already been married two years, and I knew and felt my time to become a mother was coming soon.

In fact, prior to leaving, Chris and I had planned to visit family and friends in the States in 2020 after our two years were up, before signing another contract. When discussing with my family the possibilities of where to meet, and what to do, Chris and I shared that we felt we probably wouldn't be coming home just the two of us, and that might play a role in where we go. At the time, we were in discussion with each other about adoption, or having our own children by blood. Then, while we were in Las Montañas, we were given the opportunity to attend an international YWAM Together conference in another country, which required us to travel by bus, plane, and bus again. On our return, I was exhausted from the long day of travel, and was drifting in and out of consciousness much like the rest of the riders with me in the over six-hour van ride back to our little village. I had experienced much spiritual growth during our time at the conference, and I wanted to continue that growth, so I was determined to be devoted to spending the journey in quiet prayer and reflection. I had prayed and listened seemingly about everything, when I randomly started praying about becoming a mother. In prayer, I felt that the Lord was going to move in that area of my life very soon. I couldn't get the words, "By Mother's Day," out of my head, so I prayed for Him to prepare my heart if this were to be true. Then, I finally succumbed to exhaustion and slept the rest of the journey.

While I was writing my previous book, I was younger in marriage, and neither my husband nor I felt ready for me to be expecting. Of course, I was born to be a mommy, but it wasn't the right time. However, at the time of the microchimerism teaching in Word by Heart that impacted me so deeply, it became very evident that I no longer feared being pregnant. So, one night, shortly after that teaching, Chris and I were finally *fully* intimate as husband and wife. After a couple of times that month, I began to feel more and more that what we were doing as husband and wife was right. Then, it happened.

I was feeling nauseated, and I had to go to the restroom at least every hour! *Was I pregnant?!* As the time drew closer for Aunt Flow (my period, for those of you who don't understand the nickname) to arrive, I began exhibiting more and more "symptoms." Chris and I began speaking with some of our leaders about this possibility of me being pregnant, and when to test, etc. *Wow, it was becoming so real!* We were nervous, excited, terrified, filled with joy, and so many other emotions. For the past five years or so, Aunt Flow visited me very regularly, never late, never early, and exactly seven to eight days minimum. So, Chris and I excitedly bought pregnancy tests when I was a day late, and I took one very early in the morning when it was two days late. Negative. *Well, Las Montañas didn't have the most advanced tests like in the States, so I guess I'll wait.* And then she came. Two days late in the afternoon, with a vengeance. That day, I had never before been more devastated, and I cried on and off for two days straight, and then for the rest of the month at random times. I felt ridiculous. *How could I be so upset over something I wasn't sure I wanted just yet?* But I prayed with Chris, my leaders, and others, and determined that yes, we were ready to try, and my heart was ready to love a baby, *my* baby.

The next month, we actually tracked my cycle and tried for a baby. We were graduating from our school when I was due for a visit from Aunt Flow. This time, I was not going to get my hopes up until she didn't arrive after five days! To my utter surprise, she never came! I took a test, and my life changed forever with those two little pink lines!

Wow! I'm going to be a mommy, just like that! We told our family and close friends right away because we knew that the first trimester of a pregnancy is the most difficult, and the most dangerous, so we wanted all the prayers we could get. Everyone was ecstatic, and we all began planning and dreaming of our future with our family of three!

Some people don't ever want to be parents, and they become terrified of those two lines. Some people have always wanted to be parents. That was me. I was *born* to be a mommy! I always figured I would adopt instead of having my own because I was terrified of the birth pain, but when I became pregnant, I imagined seeing my little baby on the sonogram, hearing her heartbeat for the first time, feeling her kicks, and sitting in the hospital holding my baby for the first time. I couldn't imagine why I had ever been so fearful. Yes, the first trimester would be difficult, and so would *actually* giving birth, but I have always heard that it was all worth it when you hold your baby for the first time. I couldn't wait! August 10th couldn't come soon enough!

When I was just over a month pregnant, Chris and I had to travel to another country for a visa run, something all-too familiar for global missionaries. While we were there in our visa-run country, I experienced morning sickness, fatigue, extreme sensitivity to smell, and my first scare.

One night, I specifically had a nightmare that the enemy in the form of a demon had targeted and attacked my baby. It was the same demon we had encountered in reality just weeks prior to discovering I was pregnant. I woke up, rebuked all these things, and prayed over my sweet baby. After prayer, and reassurance from my leaders, I felt more at ease. And the symptoms continued to increase. When we suspected that I was about eight weeks pregnant, we scheduled an appointment with the local doctor.

The visit was *nothing* like the movies and TV shows aired. I had to first get a prescription from the OBGYN to have a blood test and an ultrasound. Then, I had to walk to another building, about a block away, and sit and wait for the lab technician to arrive. I was told beforehand to not use the restroom until after my lab work, so I held it. In these countries, doctors and medical professionals get up whenever it is convenient for them, and you as the patient wait...and wait...and wait. I waited for at least three hours. *Hasn't anyone heard not to make a pregnant woman hold her bladder?* Finally, the technician arrived and started taking patients. There was only one problem. Though I had been the first in line, this country served whoever came to the cloth curtain first. Many other women pushed and shoved their way in front of me, and I was feeling disheartened. So, after explaining my case, the technician finally told me to enter behind the curtain. But Chris had to wait outside the room. The technician slathered on the ultrasound gel and rubbed my belly for about two minutes. Then, the nurse told me to go to the restroom and return. I did, and this time, the technician rubbed my belly for three minutes, took pictures, and sent me away. He never spoke a word to me until he instructed me to return back after 3 pm for the results. Needless to say, I was emotional because he never indicated my baby was okay. He never let me see the screen, and he never said, "There's your baby!" which was always done in television shows and movies. I never had the opportunity to see that hazy weather map most people call it with my tiny peanut in the middle.

We returned to the OBGYN hours later with results in hand, and the report stating I had been about six weeks pregnant, not eight, like we originally thought. The doctor had examined all the lab work and directed me to return to our doctor in Las Montañas in two weeks for a more accurate scan. The baby was simply too young to see her little peanut figure.

When we returned to Las Montañas in January, we scheduled an appointment for almost exactly two weeks after we had seen the doctor in our visa-run country. We were hoping to see our little one on the ultrasound, and possibly hear her heartbeat. After all, she'd be about eight weeks by now. In the meantime, while we waited for the appointment, one of the friends we had made in our Word by Heart school helped me to start making a quilt for my baby. It helped me pass the time, so I did not become too impatient. We went to the market to purchase the perfect material, and she reminded me how to use a sewing machine. My grandmother had taught me how to sew many years prior, and I imagined teaching my daughter to do the same, explaining how I had relearned while making her little quilt. My friend and I poured hours into making this quilt, which was to be the start of many homemade items from the mission field for my sweet little baby.

Then, finally the time arrived to see our little peanut, who would *definitely* be large enough to see, and to hopefully hear the heartbeat. This time, Chris *was* allowed into the ultrasound room, and I thank God he was. I couldn't have faced the impending devastating news if he wasn't there. The doctor searched for over six horrid minutes before coming to the conclusion that my baby was not growing and would *never* grow anymore. She suggested I schedule a D&C right away to "clean me out." "But I am still having all the symptoms!" I sobbed. Chris was holding me tightly against his chest as I was soaking his shirt with my tears. The technician decided I could safely wait another week to make sure her findings were accurate, so we did. I was still weeping in the bustling hospital front room as we waited for a taxi to come and pick us up. Chris was using his best language skills and trying to talk to anyone who could help us.

Meanwhile, I was a puddle in the ground, surrounded by curious on-lookers who didn't understand why this foreigner was making such a scene. I didn't care. My world had stopped. A woman whom I had never met before that day or seen after that day came to me and embraced me tightly. She disclosed that she was a believer (a public confession that could *easily* have landed her in jail), and she simply hugged me, comforted me, and prayed for me in her language while Chris finally hailed a taxi. Oftentimes when I allow myself to return my thoughts to that moment, I wonder *was she an angel sent by the Lord to comfort me?* I returned back to the place we called home in Las Montañas and continued to weep uncontrollably. Chris did his best to soothe me, and to pray. He was confused but trying to remain strong for us. I quickly fell asleep, exhausted from grief.

I can now relate to the disciples on the Mount of Olives who fell asleep when Jesus asked them to pray. No matter how hard I tried to fight to stay awake to pray, I gave into the exhaustion. When I awoke hours later, Chris and another woman who had been living in the house with us, began telling me to play worship music for the baby and to pray, refusing to accept the diagnosis of the technician. This was the first of many glimpses of hope I had received that dreadful week. We all prayed, Chris fasted, and together, we worshiped the Lord. After that, we all felt that the baby was simply too young for this sub-par technology. Or perhaps my baby was camera-shy. So, I continued making that quilt as a way to combat the doctor's words, and in faith that this baby would use this quilt in about six-to-seven more months.

Soon after that, my parents came to visit on their way home from a trip to Norway, and their suitcases were filled with goodies for the little baby, who should have been about ten to eleven weeks old at that time. Hope was fully restored to all of us as my symptoms persisted, and as we remained in prayer together. I began dreaming of the technician seeing our little miracle baby, and me being able to tell her about the powerful God we served. In our prayer time, we had also been praying for stronger symptoms to confirm this baby was healthy. And the Lord answered our prayers...or so we thought.

While out shopping and sightseeing with my parents, I hit a wall. I began feeling absolutely exhausted, and then nauseated. I couldn't hold it in any longer, so my dad asked for some plastic bags from a shop owner, and my lunch emptied into them. *This was a great sign!* We had finished our shopping and sightseeing, so we returned to our home. I began getting sick around 2 pm and did not stop until about 8 pm when I then proceeded to dry heave until about 11 pm. I was incredibly weak but determined to drink rehydration packets and keep my strength up for this baby. While I was dry heaving, Chris and my parents had been praying and talking, and it was determined that it would be best if I came home to the States, received a healthy diagnosis, heard the heartbeat so we could stop worrying, and then returned to the global mission field. We were going to be heading to another country in April anyway, we were experiencing snags with our visa plans, and we had been secretly warned that the government was sending spies to catch missionaries in the act. Just two months after leaving, the regional leader was indeed arrested for his work as a missionary due to spies catching him. The base with which we were staff had been contemplating sending home most of the foreigners as our presence really called attention to ourselves. *So, we might as well leave slightly earlier than expected.*

The next day, my health and strength had returned! My color had been restored to my face, I had finished vomiting, and it was as if the previous events of the day had never *actually* happened. Except they had, and now we had to begin packing. Some who were living with us were concerned that I was not fit to fly, but God had led Chris and my parents to book plane tickets, and we had long enough layovers where I could get rest and medical help if needed. So, off we went.

Just before leaving Las Montañas, I started spotting. My mom, and many pregnancy apps reassured me that stress could have triggered it, and as long as it remained brown or light pink, I was okay and so was the baby. But it didn't. It darkened and began looking bright red as we neared the United States. I began to panic, but I was determined to keep meditating on Bible verses and stories we had learned, and I continued to believe this experience was going to help me in finally overcoming fear. I was going to reach a new depth of faith. When purchasing last-minute plane tickets, Chris had unknowingly bought first-class tickets as they were the only ones available at the time, but they were highly discounted, costing barely more than a regular economy ticket. With this, we were allowed to rest in the first-class lounge, eating as much as we could during our long layover. We found a comfortable spot in a quiet corner, then I fell asleep smiling with the hope that we would be able to tell our baby one day about the time she helped us accidentally fly first class.

Chris and I had already decided to go to the hospital the same day that we landed in Las Vegas to hear the baby's heartbeat so I wouldn't have to *continue* worrying. By this time, it was as if my period had returned. When we landed, my parents were still a flight away as they had already booked different tickets before we decided to fly home. They were on a layover waiting for their last flight, so I called my mom and explained what was happening. I asked her if my baby was okay, but in my heart, I knew she wasn't. My mom suggested we check into the hotel, then get to the hospital right away instead of waiting for them to arrive, as was the original plan. Chris didn't want to have to face this again alone, but it began to look like he had no other choice.

After we checked into the hotel, groggy from the trip, and filled with worry, we made our way to the labor and delivery section of the hospital. That's where they treated pregnant women in Las Montañas, so we figured that was where I should have gone in the hospital in the States. However, the secretaries took one look at me, and coldly directed me to go to make an appointment at a women's clinic. Then I told them I was bleeding and needed to see a doctor right away. So, they sent me to the ER. After waiting for what seemed like hours, I saw the ultrasound technician who, yet again, would not let my worried, jet-lagged husband be in the room with me.

At this time, there was still hope that I would hear my baby's heartbeat, but it was fleeting as the minutes ticked by. The technician's face was stone, and completely un-telling as she conducted the ultrasound. Even through all the fear, I was telling her I could not wait to hear the heartbeat and see the ultrasound. She replied with something to the effect of, "Right now the baby might still be too small, and for privacy, I cannot show you the ultrasound." Then, I was reunited with my husband, and we waited again until the doctor finally entered. With a smile on her face, she diagnosed me with a bladder infection, and then said to prepare to have a miscarriage. She said matter-of-factly that this was really common, and there was only a 1% chance I wouldn't lose the baby. There was no sensitivity, no compassion, not even, "I'm so sorry," nothing but devastating news and a *huge* hospital bill. I was too defeated to protest that I still had all the symptoms. We left the hospital knowing that our dreams of holding our precious baby on this side of eternity were absolutely demolished. This was Thursday evening.

My parents arrived at the hotel about twenty minutes after we returned from the hospital, and everything surrounding that was foggy. I don't remember if I told them we had lost the baby, or if they had figured it out themselves, but I do know that I sobbed every moment I was awake that night. Sometime that night, I blinked back the tears enough to post on Facebook that we had lost our sweet baby, but everything surrounding that is such a blur in my memory. Again, I fell asleep, exhausted from grief. Friday morning, we all awoke early, packed our things, and traveled home to Lake Havasu, mainly in silence. I was incredibly numb, unable to cry any more tears as they had all been cried...or so I thought. When we returned to my childhood home, I made a beeline straight to the bed in my brother's room-turned guest room, and I wept again, hoping, praying to wake up from this awful nightmare. But I never did, and unfortunately, I never will. My nightmare became my reality and I needed to learn how to live with my grief. We did our best after arriving to resume "normal" lives. After all, Chris and I had returned home to family and friends after over six months away. People wanted to see us. We wanted to see them. Plus, we wanted to get going on outreach for Word by Heart and prepare for our next journey back to the global mission field.

That Saturday, Alena and David, some of our closest friends, and Rita, my childhood best friend, made a last-minute three and a half-hour trip from Phoenix to Lake Havasu to see Chris and me. Our plan was to tell our Word by Heart stories to them and simply spend time together, enjoying each others' company. We also wanted to attend church as much as we could while home since we hadn't heard many sermons in English in the time we were away, and we probably wouldn't hear many more when we returned to the global mission field. Plus, we wanted to give back to our community, so we decided to intentionally make our relationships with the bodies of various local churches stronger. As a group, we all went to a church service on Saturday night, joined by another of our close friends, April. That was a big mistake.

By this time, it was February, so generally, sermons revolved around love, or at least they had the tendency to do so. This particular church had begun a series on none other than parenting and families. After worship, when I glimpsed the title, I scrambled clumsily out of my chair, flew past all my friends out to the reception area, and began weeping once again. Chris followed behind, and so did Rita. He held our friends' car keys in hand as the three of us marched straight to the car so I could escape from the rest of the world and cry. After church, however, Alena, David, Rita, and April opened up the door for Chris and me to talk about what we needed to. They didn't give any suggestions, any "at least" statements, any personal stories turning the attention on them, etc. They simply listened, cried, and prayed.

Sunday morning, we returned to my childhood church, Christ Chapel, formerly known as Community Presbyterian Church-ECO (CPC), and Chris and I were overwhelmed with those who weren't on Facebook asking when I was due and congratulating us on our baby. My parents, Rita, and a couple of other members of the church tried to cut people off and let them know the situation before they could say anything, but most of the time, they were too late. As if that weren't triggering enough, some women from our local pregnancy center had been scheduled to speak and present to our church *that* Sunday. In my history of faithfully attending church most Sundays, I have no memory of ever hearing from women from the Pregnancy Center. Thankfully, my pastor had graciously called previously to warn me, so I knew my sign to leave when the two women walked up to the front to speak. I sprinted past all the churchgoers as if my life depended on it. I burst through the front doors, then melted to the ground outside, overtaken with so much grief. My mom had been assigned the task of informing me when the presentation was finished, and it was safe to enter again, so she remained, her heart torn, wanting nothing more than to run after me.

I could have remained melted on the concrete forever, but God sent Alena's father to gently pick me up in a way I knew my Heavenly Father was acting through him. Then, he handed me off to my mom and another incredible sister in Christ who simply hugged me and cried with me. When I had regained my strength, we all walked into the church and faced the congregation, who had been made aware of our present state, and why I reacted in such a way. We walked past the baby bottles that were left so that the members could raise money for the pregnancy center. My heart wanted to grab one, but my hand couldn't bear to touch any. At the end of the service, however, I felt irritatingly compelled to speak with Debbie and Denise from Pregnancy Care. I approached the pair, and barely managed to squeak, "Do you offer miscarriage counseling?" I think when I said this, the world stopped as all the people tasked with the duty of protecting me from well-meaning people stood still in their tracks. Debbie agreed silently, then slipped a business card in my hand and offered a compassionate hug. Tears burst forth from my eyes once again.

Sunday night Rita offered to spend the night, and I am eternally grateful she did. I hadn't slept well since Friday night, and I often found myself in and out of hot baths to try to soothe the intense cramps I was experiencing. That night, I had taken three baths, then after the third, I never made it off the bathroom floor to dry off, get dressed, and return to my room. I was writhing in agony. I was weeping from the emotional pain and screaming from the physical pain. I've experienced my fair share of agonizing pain, but on a scale of one to ten, my pain was fifty that night. I managed to climb onto the toilet and felt the overwhelming urge to push. I proceeded to give birth to my little one. I never got to experience the "it was worth it" feeling while holding my baby in my arms, gazing lovingly at her face. What happened next is still very blurry as I was sleep-deprived, still writhing in pain, and now realizing the extent of what had actually happened. Plus, I have intentionally blocked it from my memory as what I did has me ridden with so much guilt.

I covered myself with a towel, cleaned myself up as much as I could, and woke Rita up. I couldn't stand the thought of seeing Chris' agony, looking at what was left of our lifeless baby, and he hadn't slept well since returning home to the States, so I didn't dare wake him. Regret number one; I wish I had given him the chance to make the decision for himself of what to do. Rita prayed with me, and then I called my mom, as I was unable to move. I wanted to collect the remains, *but what would I do with them?* My appointment wasn't until tomorrow, later in the morning, and it was quite late at night. I held the sack, my baby, in my hands, cried silently, then at the advice of the two women with me, I laid her body to rest eternally and flushed: regret number two. I wish I had saved her remains and cremated them or buried them. Even now, as I see friends who have suffered the same thing wearing rings and jewelry made from their babies' ashes, I can't help but feel regret. I have been so consumed with guilt that I did this, and this guilt has consumed so many other mothers who had no other choice. I want to address you with the same thing I have been told time and time again, your baby was already in Heaven, in the arms of the One who had adopted him or her. What was flushed was just a shell. It does not make you a bad mother, nor one who has to live with this guilt. No one can imagine the situation until it happens to him or her, so there is no way to prepare. There is no *right* thing to do.

Monday morning, I was numb yet again. The end of the physical pain was finally in reach, and once it was reached, my body could heal, then my heart, then my soul. I went to the OBGYN, completed the paperwork, then emotionlessly stated to the secretary, "It doesn't really matter. I passed my baby last night." She gave me her condolences, then hurried me to see the doctor. It was as if she knew the misery I was feeling as each swollen belly walked past me in the waiting room. Chris and I went into the exam room, hoping for the best, the impossible. *Perhaps the hospital and all the other doctors were wrong. Perhaps what I had passed the night before was not our baby, and she still had a chance.* I know, these thoughts were as false as the idea that I would eventually wake up from this nightmare, but they were all I had. *Maybe we were having twins, and one survived?* None of these thoughts obviously materialized. However, I felt relieved when the doctor told me that most of the remains had been cleared out naturally. She prescribed medication to finish the physical healing, and clear out everything instead of performing a D&C. For that, I was eternally grateful.

The medication was supposed to induce labor, and I was told it would be incredibly painful, so my doctor also prescribed pain medication and then anti-nausea medicine for that. I prepared to stay in all day for the next two days, thinking the worst was yet to come. To my shock and relief, the pain I had experienced Sunday night/Monday morning was so much greater than what the medication caused. It was as if I was having only slight period cramps; I had experienced much more painful cramps before in many of my cycles. I never touched the other two medications, and for the first time since this process had begun, I felt an ounce of peace that the healing was about to begin. When I returned for a checkup the next week, my hopes were confirmed. I felt very guilty that I was grateful that everything that physically had resulted from my pregnancy with my baby had been naturally cleansed from my body. I hated myself for the relief, but again, my relief was not that my baby was gone, but that healing could finally begin. I was also incredibly thankful that *this* doctor was completely opposite to the ER doctor. She teared up with me, embraced me, reassured me, and told me to let myself heal in my own time. She even reaffirmed that I *did* indeed lose my baby, and no matter how young that baby was, it was still incredibly painful and I *did* need to allow myself to grieve.

***

Chris:

Just before we left for our visa-run country, I was also attacked one night. Late into the evening while everyone slept, I was awoken by the sound of demons chanting and when I opened my eyes I couldn't move. All I could see was a dark figure in the corner of our small bedroom and then in a moment it was looming over Denelle and I in our bed. All I could do was scream in my mind and spirit, "Come, Lord Jesus!" And in the next moment I saw a flash of light above us wrestle with the darkness and then both were gone, and I was able to move.

While we were staying in the country for our visa run, I was hopelessly naive, and thought nothing more of the nightmare experience. We shared Word by Heart stories in churches, with the Salvation Army, and with a fancy dining room full of non-believers on Christmas Eve. *We were working for the Lord, and everything was going to be ok, right?* Then Christmas morning came. I awoke in our small room. It was so cold outside that the walls were sweating. We were supposed to attend church that morning with our host and his family, but Denelle had become sick. So, instead, we spent that Christmas in a tiny room together and watched movies all day while Denelle tried to keep down crackers and water. Through her bouts of sickness and sleep, I prayed, "Please, just keep them safe."

I vaguely remember the day that Denelle went to the doctor while we were away. There wasn't much I could do to be there for her as the doctors wouldn't let me go into the room with her. All I could do was sit out in the waiting room and pray. Normally that would be enough for me, but at that moment, I felt completely helpless. She handed me her things, we exchanged glances, and then I waited. When it comes to my wife's health, I can be irritable and pushy at times. At regular intervals, I would go to the counter and ask if she'd been seen yet, or when they were *actually* going to do something for her. The answer was always the same, "Please wait; she will be seen soon." I never felt more useless. I never got to see an ultrasound, or even be with Denelle.

Hosanna! Hosanna is coming! These words would echo in my mind as we awaited to see what was to come regarding our little peanut. We stood outside of the small church in Las Montañas, and the words rang clear. Denelle's parents had come to see us, and we had just gotten out of church when I first heard it. I remember exactly where I stood. At the time, I only interpreted the phrase that we would praise the Lord in due time, and I thought it was meant for the baby we were currently expecting. Later, I would come to believe that the phrase would mean that even in our hurt, we would praise Him.

Denelle's parents weren't with us long when Denelle got sick. I remember where she sat on the curb holding the bag of spaghetti dinner from the night before. She had asked for stronger pregnancy symptoms, but even then, I was nervous. I thought it was perhaps because I was a new father and didn't enjoy seeing her sick under normal circumstances. But something about her getting sick made me uneasy. *Everything was fine...right?* The color of the regurgitated dinner made me feel otherwise. I prayed instantly. *Father, please let everything be ok. Heal her and watch over her. Keep them safe.*

When we arrived back at the house in which we were staying, we were met by our two housemates, and they asked what was wrong. We informed them Denelle had gotten sick, and they prayed with us as well. They encouraged us to keep believing in God for His promises, so I began to fast and pray. It was hard to even want to. Hearing Denelle get sick for so long, I knew something was wrong and I was angry. *Why even fast? You can heal her, right? But why won't you?*

I didn't want to become angry with God, but I knew without His healing hand, nothing would change. I remember meeting with Denelle's parents without her and telling them I think it would be best for Denelle to get looked at at home before going to any other Word by Heart school. They agreed, and so I called our pastor to get his opinion and blessing on us returning home.

The entire way home I was nervous. Despite this, through the Bollywood movie bus ride, the long layover, and the taxi ride, I kept it all together on the outside. On the inside, I was a mess. I knew virtually nothing about pregnancy or what it could look like, but my wife was sick, and that was enough to make me nervous for her.

I never wanted to go to the hospital without her parents, but we needed to. Reverse culture shock sunk in as we rushed to the hospital within an hour after landing in the States for the first time in over half a year. I felt as if I had forgotten how to get a taxi, check into a hotel, or even communicate in my own language. *How would we even get to the hospital?* I didn't have a U.S. SIM card for my phone, and we didn't have cell service. Our phones were still on the SIM cards from Las Montañas. I asked the hotel clerk in the most awkward way to call a cab for us to go to the hospital, we had only been there five minutes, and now we were rushing out. "Can you...uh...call a taxi...or an ambulance for my wife? She's not feeling well." *Should she even take a taxi?*

The clerk stared at me. "Is she hurt?" I shook my head, no. She said a taxi would probably be fine and called. After what seemed like a year-and-a-half, the taxi driver arrived to take us to the hospital. *How would I even pay?* I had no U.S. currency, and our bank still thought we were overseas, so they would lock our accounts if we tried to use them. I honestly don't even remember paying.

Jet lagged and fatigued; we made our way through the hospital. I impatiently demanded for the ER receptionist to have Denelle seen ASAP. She wanted for us to wait until we got home for her to be seen by her OBGYN. Not only did we land in Las Vegas, another two-and-a-half hours away, but I pondered, *when would they even be able to see her?* My mom had set an appointment for her with an OB, but the earliest time available was Monday morning. It was Thursday.

After finally being admitted and taken to a room to wait, jet lag won me over, and I fell asleep. I awoke to the doctor or nurse telling Denelle the bad news. I don't even remember if we cried. I was too numb, tired, and angry. We waited even longer outside of the hospital ER for another ride back to the hotel. Denelle's parents were in the room waiting for us as they had arrived in the US on the flight after us. Denelle immediately went to the bathroom and cried, while I told her parents what was happening. I remember calling my dad while I stood in the hallway to ask if he could come pick us up from Vegas, realizing we didn't have a ride home. Denelle's parents had a ride because they were originally set to be picked up, just the two of them. The car wouldn't fit all of us. I cried after telling him what happened as I continued to stand in the hallway. I returned back inside after regaining myself. *How could I be there for my wife? When would Hosanna come?*

"O Lord, you have examined my heart and know everything about me."

(Psalm 139:1 NLT)

Your Turn: It's in the darkest times that light can shine its brightest. Take time to reflect on the journey that brought you here. Let the Lord reveal even the darkest parts of your heart so that healing may come.

4

Spontaneous Abortion

Abortion is a word that fuels much debate and passion from both those who are pro-life and pro-choice. Politics are not part of the purpose of this book, but those two words off the page on my medical discharge papers after losing my baby added salt to my very fresh wound. I had never heard of the term "spontaneous abortion" before, so I protested with my ER doctor when she brought the offensive packet to me. "I didn't *choose* an abortion. I lost my baby!" The doctor coldly replied with, "That's the medical term."

Abortion simply means, "the termination of a pregnancy after, accompanied by, resulting in, or closely followed by the death of the embryo or fetus: such as a spontaneous expulsion of a human fetus during the first twelve weeks of gestation..." according to Merriam Webster Dictionary. However, with so much animosity surrounding the word, its connotation is that of a choice. I did not *choose* to terminate my pregnancy. Even when I was told there was no heartbeat, I did not choose this. My body simply chose for me.

In addition to the cold medical terminology, miscarriages are surrounded by guilt-induced *what-ifs. What if I ate one of the things I wasn't supposed to? What if I had just stayed in bed or at least at home instead of traveling? What if I missed a day of prenatal medicine?* The list of what-ifs seems to be endless. Whether you wanted your baby or not, you did not *choose* to endure this physical and emotional turmoil. Statistically, many miscarriages, especially early ones are not preventable, except through an act of God. There is nothing you did that caused this. There is nothing you could have done to change the outcome. It is time to put the medical terminology behind you, if that is causing the same pain it caused me. You did *not* choose this.

“Abortion.”Merriam-Webster.com.Merriam-Webster, 2024. Web. 25 March 2024.

5

Heaven-Sent Gifts

The best way I receive and show love are through gifts and affirming words. In the days and months following losing my precious baby, I received an abundance of love, especially in these forms.

No, I never received a package that was addressed from Heaven directly, but I know that the Lord put me on the senders' hearts to show His love through them to me. Each of these gifts were completely unexpected, but greatly treasured more than I can express.

1. A sister whom I had met in ministry in 2013 messaged me her story after I posted about Sammy, and she asked for my address. She directed me to the *Loved Baby* miscarriage and infant loss group on Facebook for a support group, and then mailed me a personal copy of the *Loved Baby* devotional book by Sarah

Philpott, PhD. This was the first devotional I was able to use to start coming to terms with my new reality.

2. My mom, who also shows love mostly through gifts, took me to multiple stores looking everywhere for a baby feet charm so I could craft a ring to wear in reminder and as a conversation-starter of my sweet Sammy. She recognized the importance of me having open doors to talk about my sweet baby. So, when we couldn't find any, she purchased one online for me, and then gifted me an elephant necklace to wear until the ring could be made.
3. One afternoon while I was weeping on the couch (a common occurrence for the first two months after Sammy passed) a surprise package arrived, and in it, there was a beautiful heart necklace with Sammy's due date birthstone and a message stamped, "A piece of my heart is in Heaven." It was from my Aunt Shannon simply out of love. It was later passed onto another friend whose baby celebrated their Heavenly birthday in August.
4. The next day, a card arrived in the mail from one of the members of my church. She only signed "God bless" and her name, because what was on it spoke loudly enough. It read: *We never knew or saw or touched the little miracle growing inside of you.*

   Only you knew and felt the real bond of love that grew...and has now been replaced by an aching emptiness.

   So, go ahead and grieve. Your loss is real, and the pain must seem unbearable.

   But, until your grief is softened, know that the Lord's love and comfort are there for you...and so are many prayers.
5. The day after that, I received a package from the organization, Hope Mommies. It had many precious things such as a Bible, a miscarriage Bible study book, a notebook, two bookmarks, a book about Heaven, a card, a pregnancy loss keychain, a silicone bracelet, and then some goodies for pampering myself including lotion, a candle, a bath bomb, chapstick, and some tea among

other things. This was sent by a friend whom I had met when I was in college trying to obtain all the practicum hours required for my degree. We had connected very deeply and kept in touch, but it was still such a sweet shock to know God chose to move through her to send this package to me.

6. My husband, of course, also knows gifts speak to my heart more than most other forms of love, so one night, he went with our friend on a secret mission. We had all gone to dinner together and had planned to see a movie in theaters afterward, but then grief hit me immediately following dinner. I decided I wanted to return home, while the guys would see the movie. Fortunately for me, my husband knew what I really needed, so he went to Hobby Lobby, my favorite store of all time, and got to work putting together a bin of my favorite things as well as some things he knew would simply put a smile on my face. On his way back home, he also stopped to pick up my favorite flowers. Needless to say, I melted when he returned home.
7. When Rita was over for the first weekend while I was still going through my miscarriage, she took me to the pharmacy to pick up my prescription for Cytotec. While we were there, she saw the aisle of cheesy Valentine's Day gifts, and she picked out a medium-sized stuffed elephant because she knew I loved elephants, and I needed something to hug and hold at times, especially in the days to come. This was especially important because throughout the weeks that followed, my arms *physically* ached to hold something. My body and heart knew I "had my baby" so I should have been holding her. The reality of having to wait until eternity until my arms could hold her caused an indescribable pain that only those who have endured having a child born into Heaven understand.
8. The pregnancy counselor, Debbie, gifted me a bracelet with baby feet at the gestation size of ten weeks on it, two baby feet pins, and the pregnancy package she gives to her clients when they are expecting. No, I wasn't expecting at the time, but during

my last appointment with her before moving temporarily to the Philippines, I thought I was or would be soon. She gave these gifts in faith that I would be expecting soon, while away staffing Word by Heart. Inside the package was a silicone baby at the gestation size and development of twelve weeks. It was both painful and peaceful to hold that little baby. However, I was very upset the night I received it because she was completely naked. I didn't feel right leaving her unclothed. I know, she was fake, but my mothering instinct kicked in, and I couldn't get to the store fast enough to buy something with which to swaddle her. I actually cried over that little silicone baby laying naked. But when I had finally swaddled her, and put a headband on her, I felt at peace, like I was able to do what I was supposed to do for Sammy, my baby.

9. Many others gave small gifts, whether cards or snacks, quality time, or free painting classes. I also received too many messages from friends to count. Unfortunately, many of those friends had experienced the same grief as I was experiencing, and they simply reached out to my heart. I was overwhelmed with all who stepped up. Some of whom I did not know truly cared about me until they sent their heartfelt messages.
10. God has also used many in my life to affirm me. Many had taken the time to specifically refer to me as a mother. To keep me from letting guilt overtake me, they continuously declared truth over me. Additionally, they reassured me that they were praying for our family, and for our rainbow baby.

While these may seem to be trivial things to some, everything on my list and off of it has been used by the Lord to show me that He has not forgotten me, and that He dearly loves me. These gifts, and the way the community had formed around me, told me that I was seen, I was loved, and that it was okay to grieve.

***

Chris:

I usually receive love differently than my wife, but I did give a few gifts to myself. During our time at home after losing Sammy, I got her name tattooed on my left arm in Las Montañas' script. No, it doesn't say something weird like some people's Chinese tattoos that look really deep, but really only mean, "soup." While in Las Montañas, Denelle and I learned how to read and write in the script and so I do know it says her name. Then, after the loss of our second baby, I got Micah's name tattooed on my right arm while we were living in Cambodia. The mark they left is permanently on my heart, and now also permanently in my skin. These tattoos serve as reminders, as well as open doors to start a conversation, no matter how uncomfortable it may be at times. Each permanent mark was a step toward healing for me, and I encourage other fathers to find something they can keep as a reminder of not just something they lost, but of God's ultimate promise. What we lose, God will restore.

Some days I forget I have them, and other days, I see my tattoos as if for the first time and I take a moment of silence from the world as I reflect on my two children who are waiting for me when this life is said and done. These tattoos also remind me to cherish the two kids that I do have here, even when they aren't listening, or perhaps giving their mommy and me a hard time. I gain perspective. We could not have either of *them* as well, and I just don't think my heart could bear that. So, these names remind me, not always of what I lost, but what I now have. They remind me at times to put down my phone, stop being so busy, and just enjoy the two miracles that call me "Daddy". Other than spending time with Jesus, nothing could be more important. The tattoos stay in my skin and never seem to fade. They're silent, yet they speak to me everyday.

Your Turn: When do you feel most loved? Reflect on how others have done things specifically to reach out and comfort you.

6

Naming Sammy

About a week after giving birth to our baby, my church hosted an event which welcomed Pastor Todd Burpo, the author of *Heaven is For Real.* To prepare for the event, Chris, my parents, and I decided to watch the movie, which is very close to the details in the book. I hadn't seen it yet, or read the book, but the others had many years back. However, no one remembered to warn me about what I was going to watch. The movie follows young Colton, who had gone to Heaven in what some describe as a near-death experience. He returned to Earth/ life as an answer to his father's prayers, but he returned as a completely changed boy. After the experience, Colton began slowly relaying to his family details of Heaven. One particular detail was that he met his older sister. Colton never knew his mom had had a miscarriage, but while in Heaven, his sister came up to him and hugged him. "She wouldn't stop hugging me," he claimed. When he told his mom he had another sister, she began asking about her. When she asked what her name was, Colton told her that she didn't have a name because they didn't name her. It was at this moment in the movie Chris left the room, and I began to sob once again. They hadn't named her because, much like Sammy, Colton's sister entered eternity too early to know the gender. It was at that moment I determined I didn't want an unnamed baby in Heaven.

So, I began praying. Then Chris too began praying. The next day, I spoke with Chris, and we decided to name our baby, Sammy. It was a gender-neutral name, since we didn't *truly* know whether our baby was a boy or girl, but in prayer, we have always felt she was a girl. The name Sammy was based on the biblical character of Samuel. In the story of Samuel, Hannah wept for many years, praying for a child to bear. When the Lord answered her requests, she named the boy, Samuel, meaning "asked of God" or "heard by God" because she said in 1 Samuel 1:27, "For this child, I have prayed, and the LORD has granted me my petition which I asked of Him." Chris and I had never before prayed more for anything or anyone in our life than for Sammy at that point. It was only fitting to give her such a namesake.

While watching *Heaven is For Real* helped Chris and I decide to name our baby, I was now even more nervous about attending the speaking event, but my mom suggested it might be healing for us. She was right. It was, but in general, healing is painful, and it was indeed very painful. I had braced myself for the topic of them losing their baby to come up, but not enough. My pastor had even forewarned me about the strong likelihood of this topic arising in the question-and-answer session. He had actually expressed to me that if I felt it was going to be too painful, then he would talk to Mr. Burpo about going around that topic as the wound was still too fresh. While my flesh craved this, my heart knew it needed healing, and healing would not come if others tiptoed around the topic. So, I reluctantly declined the offer.

The first third of the question-and-answer session was great, and very eye-opening! But, the second third was so painful to me, that I almost missed the last third. Mr. Burpo began by recapping what had been described in both the book, and in the movie when Colton relayed to his mom that he had a sister in Heaven. At this part in the presentation, Mr. Burpo addressed all the parents who had lost children in pregnancy, pleading with them to name their babies. He also admitted that he and his wife could not agree on a name, so they have decided that whoever goes to Heaven first gets to name their daughter. Then, Burpo decided to release a detail which had not been in the movie. He said that Colton stated matter-of-factly that God the Father had *adopted* all the babies who had died in their mothers' wombs. (Since we were discussing specifically pregnancy and infant loss at this point, he did not address other children who were grown, and then died). It was this particular detail, which sent me flying through the congregation to the church "cry room" (or room women could go to if their children were fussy) to weep once again. My glasses had fogged up from my tears so I could not see who else was with me, but I do know my mom and the other member of our church who had been with me before followed me into that room. Another member joined also, and simply prayed over the three of us. I still don't know why, but I had felt so overwhelmed by the fact that God the Father had adopted my baby. After what seemed like an eternity of weeping, praying, hugging, and repeating the process over again, we all rejoined the session to listen to the rest of what Mr. Burpo wanted to relay to us.

Once finished, in the same humble spirit with which he had presented himself to us the entire evening, Mr. Burpo offered to stay as late into the night to pray with anyone who wanted to pray with him, no matter how long it took. Of course, I immediately looked at Chris and my parents straight in the eyes and told them I needed to pray, though they didn't need any verbal confirmation as they already knew this fact. So, we waited in line.

When it was my time to approach Mr. Burpo, I didn't have to say anything. I had been sitting in the front of the church, so he had obviously witnessed me making my not-so-stealthy escape. He simply said, "I am so sorry for your loss," then he asked if he could pray with us. I nodded my head silently. He asked if we had named our baby, and if we knew what gender our baby was. We told him we named our baby, Sammy, and were inspired to do so after we watched his movie. Then we said that our baby was too young to know if he or she was a boy or girl. He prayed over me, over the pain I was experiencing, and for the healing I so desperately desired. All the time he was praying, he kept saying "she" and "her." We never needed to tell him that we all felt Sammy was a baby girl, and that some of us had seen dreams of her. He was just praying the way the Holy Spirit led him. Then, my dad asked him to pray for Chris, Sammy's grieving dad. When he did, he reaffirmed Chris's faith and strength, and also gave us hope that we would definitely have living children in the future, but that we were indeed parents to our baby in Heaven *now.*

Little did I know, my own parents were also inspired to name their baby in Heaven. After I was born, I had another little sibling who passed in my mom's womb before my living brother, Austin, was born. In various times throughout experiencing our pain, God was also opening up my parents' old wounds, which had never fully been healed until now. It seemed that as Chris and I underwent our healing, so did my parents. After this particular event, in addition to seeing my family members and friends I have lost, I have the hope of meeting at least two people who had never lived on Earth: my beautiful baby, Sammy, and my little brother, Joey.

***

Chris:

Has anyone welcomed you into parenthood, even though you may not have a child here on Earth? As we waited to leave for the Philippines, we were visited at our local church by Todd Burpo. During that time my wife was in the thick of her grief and pain. I did everything I could to help her, without dealing fully with my own hurt. It was during this time that I was welcomed into the ever-growing clan of parents. I stood next to my wife as she spoke with Todd, and he prayed for her to ultimately have peace. I remember praying with them, and not feeling much. After we exchanged our gratitude for Todd's time, my father-in-law spoke up. I remember it clearly as if it were yesterday. He placed a hand on my shoulder and asked if Todd would pray for me as well. "Can we pray for the hurting father, also?" His words rang clear. They all huddled around me and placed their hands on me to pray. It was such a small request, but it lifted a weight I had been carrying and I felt acknowledgment that I didn't even know I needed. I was truly overwhelmed to be thought of in that manner, and I do wonder if perhaps Denelle's dad speaking up for me was something he wished someone had done for him.

I encourage you, mothers and fathers, to pray for one another, and welcome each other. We certainly welcome you into this crazy clan called "parenthood." We see you, whether your children are in Heaven, Earth, or both!

Your turn: If you have already given your baby a name, what is the meaning of that name? If you have not, and you feel comfortable, take time now to pray about a name for your little one in Heaven.

7

Where was God?

I want to clarify something. In this entire process I never felt like God took my baby, or that He was to blame. I never felt angry with Him. Confused? Of course. I know and have experienced my Lord's miraculous healing in my life and in others'. *Why didn't He choose to heal my baby?* I probably will never know on this side of eternity, but I do firmly believe that it was not God's will that my baby be born into Heaven. I don't believe in a God who would give us this much joy in our very first baby, just to take her away at only six weeks gestation (an age most doctors don't believe there is actually a baby), yet I carried her for twelve to thirteen weeks. I don't believe He needed her, or that He needed another angel. In fact, there is no biblical evidence to support people turning into angels once they die. The Bible says in Hebrews 1:14 that angels are ministering spirits sent out for the sake of the believers (paraphrased version). In 1 Corinthians, Paul writes that we will judge angels. So why would I want my little baby to become an angel? I know she's in her glorified body, basking in the Lord's holy presence. I do believe God had plans for my daughter, and that these plans did not cease just because she entered her eternal home. I believe something happened to my little girl, an attack or something, and God, the Father chose to bring her home with Him.

Even though I never felt anger, only confusion, and grief, I still felt very, very abandoned by my God. Did He ever leave me? No. But my grief created a cloud that could not be penetrated in my heart. That cloud blocked me from feeling His presence and hearing His tender whispers. That all changed when I had a prayer session scheduled with another believer, I had met at a YWAM Together conference. This prayer time was very healing, but the best part was that the Lord desired to show me where He was. He wanted to answer *that* question in my heart at least. To do this, He brought me back to those places I so wanted to forget.

When I first discovered I was pregnant, He was there. I saw Him rejoicing with Chris and me and placing His hand upon my stomach to pray blessings over Sammy. He obviously wasn't surprised, just genuinely joyful for this new life growing within me and for us to experience this joy as well.

When we were leaving Las Montañas, He was there. He was sitting between Chris and me, praying over sweet Sammy's first trip. When we arrived in our visa-run country, He was there making sure I never ate or drank anything that would make me sick or harm the baby. When I awoke from my nightmare, He was there, silently crying, praying for strength and faith to wash over me. He went to our first appointment, rubbing my shoulders this time to calm me down. When I was having my lab work, He was holding my hand, tears forming in His eyes at the pain He knew was about to ensue. When we had the results read by the doctor, He was whispering into the doctor's ear to give us hope that the baby was still too young; it wasn't our time to know yet. When we returned to Las Montañas, He was there. He gave me joy again to start making a quilt, to buy some things for our sweet baby, and to dream of our future again. Then, when we were told at the hospital that the baby would never grow again, He was there, holding both Chris and me, weeping with us. Then, He whispered to me not to get a D&C. He knew I wouldn't have been able to live with myself if I had. I needed confirmation that she had passed into His arms, and I wouldn't get it yet. I would always be plagued by the what-ifs. He was there in the hospital waiting room as Chris was desperately trying to arrange for a taxi. He sent a believer (and there are very few in Las Montañas and in the hospital) to my side to comfort me and to hug me. I don't ever recall seeing or meeting her before or after that moment, but she seemed to know me. *Could she have been an angel?* When we arrived at the place we called, "home," He was there, whispering hope into my heart, and the hearts of all others with us at that time. It still wasn't our time to grieve. He was there while I was continuing to make the quilt in faith that she was okay. He was there, rejoicing with us as my parents had made the journey to visit us.

When I was throwing up, He was simultaneously giving me the strength to keep hydrated, while also in the meeting with my parents and Chris, leading them to make the decision to return home so that we would be among family and friends who could be comforting to us. He was there when I began spotting while traveling, whispering hope and His Word into my heart. He knew it would be time for me to grieve soon. He was there when we rushed to the hospital after landing in Las Vegas, holding Chris' and my hands. He was there, hurt by the lack of sensitivity when the doctor was so uncompassionate in giving her diagnosis. He was there, simply pulling my hair out of my face, rubbing my back, and strengthening my family to help us when I was in a fog the rest of the night. He was there, hating how much it hurt me, crying for me, His daughter, rubbing my back each time I was writhing in pain on the bathroom floor. He was there, letting Rita, my mom, and me know when I held the sack that Sunday night that Sammy had already gone to be with Him over six weeks ago.

He was there, telling the secretary at the OBGYN office to get me in as quickly as possible to the exam room, and He was there, telling the doctor to handle everything sensitively. He was there at the second appointment, telling me that my physical healing could begin, relieved as I soon would be. He couldn't stand seeing His children in so much pain. He was there drying my tears each time I burst out crying, and He sent people to send me messages, visit me, send me gifts, etc. As the numbness faded, and I began to accept what had happened, He was whispering to me that Sammy never knew evil, suffering, or pain. He was there the entire time.

Whether you believe what I saw in my prayer time or not, I know that the Lord wants you to seek Him. He is ready to reveal to you where He was because He was and is always there. I can honestly say that I cannot fathom going through this torturous grief process without a true and living relationship with the Lord. There are many reasons to be thankful to Him, but I am truly grateful that because of Christ's sacrifice, I can expectantly look forward to the day I meet my little Sammy for the first time. One friend once said, "You get to spend eternity getting to know Jesus and your daughter together." I now can picture myself in Heaven sitting in a meadow, listening to one of Jesus' many stories with my little daughter in my lap. Don't worry, Chris is there too, pulling her hair out her face, but Mommy gets to hold her.

Chris and I began staffing the Word by Heart school in the Philippines just a week after I had received this healing vision. I kept feeling that this particular school's "theme," if you will, was healing. When I shared openly, many others confirmed they had felt the same way. During the first week of Word by Heart: The Gospel of Luke we went through the story of the Emmaus Road. In this story, two of Jesus' disciples are returning to their homes feeling hopeless after Jesus was crucified. They unknowingly converse with Jesus Himself, who desires to bring hope to their hearts and reveal the truth to them. It is an incredible story found in Luke 24:13-36. During worship that first Friday of the school, I closed my eyes and tried to picture the story, something which is a necessary part of the process in learning the Word by Heart. However, when picturing the story, I was instead taken to the feet of Jesus as He was on the cross. This wasn't the story I wanted to picture just yet, but one I feel God wanted to show me. I was weeping at His feet due to the pain in my heart. Then, my vision panned over to the empty tomb, and I was suddenly *among* the women at the tomb. They had run off to tell the disciples what had happened, but I kept peering into the tomb which had once held my Savior's limp body. Then, Jesus tapped me on the shoulder and gave me the tightest embrace I had ever felt. I wept in His loving arms, and He simply held me. I opened my eyes again and asked God why I saw that instead of the story I was supposed to be seeing, and I felt He said to me, "Because, my precious daughter, I could not let you remain hopeless in your grief for as long as those on the road to Emmaus. I wanted to show you that I met you in your deepest grief so you would not have to walk this journey alone. You wanted my presence and believed in me, even in your feeling of hopelessness and abandonment. Those on the road to Emmaus gave up. I chose to encounter them and reveal myself to them also, just in a different way."

***

Chris:

Denelle's perspective and outlook on this time is complicated for me to understand. As her husband, all I wanted was for her to be ok. There was nothing more that I could do. I couldn't bring our baby back. I couldn't help her heart. I couldn't comfort her in any significant way. While she gained the perspective that God was with her through it all, I felt that He had remained silent. Jesus is the Author of Life, and I couldn't understand why He didn't bring this life to come to completion, not once, but twice! I don't want my faith to sound shallow or misguided. I completely relied on Jesus for everything, but at the time, I felt that my prayers weren't being heard. Even after the vision of seeing my children, I often wondered why Jesus wouldn't let Denelle see them too, when she longed to see them more than I could ever know. Then I remembered Thomas, and Jesus' reply to him. 'Blessed are those that believe without seeing'. I needed to see them and know that Jesus had taken care of our babies, and they weren't forgotten. I needed to know they were real. Denelle's faith is beautiful, and unmoving. She knew she was a mom, and she knew Jesus had them, even if she wasn't able to see them. Even though I saw my children in Jesus' arms, I was too numb to see what Denelle could. Jesus is forever faithful, and cares for the little children of the world.

'It is not your Father's will that one of these little ones should perish.'

It took years for me to see it. Jesus was there, carrying the plane smoothly across land and sea to keep us calm on the journey home. He graciously provided business seats for us to be able to rest the long journey home and provided a time of comfort. Under normal circumstances, we could never even dream of affording first class seats, but somehow managed to get them at the price of economy seating. He gave us the taxi that I didn't know how to call, our parents, friends, and speakers that would become brick and mortar in the growing wall of recovery and healing. He provided things we never asked for, and comfort in ways we could never imagine.

> "'My Lord and my God!' Thomas exclaimed. Then Jesus told him, 'You believe because you have seen me. Blessed are those who believe without seeing me.'"
>
> (John 20:28-29 NLT)

Your Turn: take time to ask Jesus to show you where He was/is in the midst of your grief. Give Him time, truly open your eyes and ears to see what He wants to show you.

8

Overcoming Jealousy & Envy

It seems that once a woman miscarries, or has experienced pregnancy loss, the entire world around her becomes pregnant. At least, that is what happened with me, and with many of the women in the online support group I take part in. Everywhere I looked, swollen bellies, newborns in strollers, the most innocent little infants flooded my reality as well as the TV shows I was watching. Even my dad remarked, "Wow! You just can't get away from this." Then, he would change the channel to something less likely to cause me pain.

Starting about a week after losing Sammy, I was *inundated* with new daily Facebook posts telling me yet another one of my friends was expecting a sweet little bundle of joy. While I *wanted* to be excited for them, I couldn't get past my grief to do so. Instead, I quickly scrolled up to move past them. *Maybe I should block them? But am I happy for them? Why can't that be me?* It took three particular women being pregnant for God to release in me the freedom to be truly joyful for the new mommies in my life.

The first was the easiest to not feel jealous over. She was a friend I had met at Grand Canyon University who also attended the same church I did when I was living in Phoenix. She still is a very kind-hearted woman with a heart after God's heart. She had been married for at least a year, maybe longer, and she was expecting. However, the problem was that her due date was simply one week after mine. Her pregnancy announcement included a beautiful ultrasound picture, which to many, looked like a peanut on a weather map. But to me, it was a reminder that I would never even have *that* of my little baby.

The next woman was due just a week before I was due to have Sammy. She was not married, not a Christian, and had made it clear many times to all who knew her growing up that she had never wanted to be a mom. Her announcement included her large dogs and a post about how unexpected things happen, that she never desired to be a mom, and that she was going to make the best of her unexpected situation.

At first, I wanted to block both of them from popping up in my newsfeed. The truth is, I couldn't stand to see them excited or nervous about the blessing I would never fully have this time around. I knew, especially as their pregnancies were progressing so beautifully and effortlessly without problems, they would be able to hold their sweet bundles of joy, both boys in August, while I would remain, longing to hold my baby. Even if I was to be expecting my rainbow baby, I still wouldn't be able to hold him or her until quite a few months after they would, and after I was hoping to. Thankfully, I never did block them, and I came to a point when I decided with God's guidance, that if I continued in this jealousy/envy, it would easily turn to bitterness. *Besides, who was I to be upset with others' happiness?* I wanted to be excited for them, and to pray blessings over them and their families. So, one night, I typed this message (it was almost the same with both women with the exception of mentions of faith):

I wanted to personally reach out to you. It's been on my mind since you announced your pregnancy, and you don't need to respond, but I wanted to share with you what I felt. Your baby is due the week before mine was, and when I saw your first bump picture, I was so jealous. You never wanted a baby, and I was BORN to be a mommy. I was very jealous, and honestly considered "unfollowing" your pregnancy journey because, to me, it just wasn't fair. I sincerely apologize for this attitude, and I want to say that I am committed to praying for your sweet baby. I am thoroughly very excited to see your bump pictures, and to see that healthy baby change your lives for the best. I'm not sure where you stand in faith matters, but if you have prayer requests, please feel free to share with me. Congratulations, and again, I apologize for my reaction. I am sincerely excited for you and your family!

The messages I received back were incredibly sincere and thoughtful. One even invited me to take part in her boy's life as much as I wanted. While I was taken aback by their responses, I was even more blessed by the freedom typing that message brought. Neither woman knew before that message that I was jealous, or that I had been wanting to block them, but for some reason, I had a nagging feeling that I *had* to confess. That night, a part of my heart turned soft again, and I decided to commit to praying for the two of them. Then, just a month later, that commitment expanded to all my friends who were expecting, especially those who had not experienced a life-changing relationship with Jesus Christ. My prayer was that as these babies were being formed by the Creator of life Himself, these moms felt the stirring in their hearts and desire to know more.

Since I was at that age, it seemed all my married friends were either pregnant, already had a little one or two, or were in a similar situation as I was, with experiencing a loss, or multiple losses. After being freed of the impending hardened heart I still sometimes experienced the temptation to get jealous of seeing perfectly round bellies, ultrasound pictures, etc. but then God reminded me that He'd already freed me from that. After that reminder, I could freely pray blessings over them again. That is, until the day my first period after losing Sammy arrived. I had typed my messages and experienced this freedom on Thursday, and my cycle began again the following Sunday.

After taking part in a couple of online support groups, I have found that periods are THE WORST after losing a baby during pregnancy. Each month, Aunt Flow rears her ugly head to remind these women, me included, we are no longer pregnant. It is especially bad when women are trying to conceive their rainbow babies only to be disappointed by her arrival. But for me, my first visit from Aunt Flow was *extra* painful.

I was in California with Chris and his family when she came. I had been crying daily still, and now I was surrounded by my sister-in-law's kids, especially her youngest, a beautiful blonde-haired girl who simply adored her mother. We were out shopping all day when I knew I needed a bathroom. Of course, I cried a lot. I texted my mom and Rita as this period just represented the finality of my pregnancy loss, and the end of all delirious hope of having a twin who was perfectly healthy (I know; it seems impossible, but I had to hold onto that idea until it was no longer even remotely possible). While all of that was awful enough, my day had barely just begun. In every store, I was once again surrounded by baby strollers or women with the baby bump I never got to experience with Sammy. Then, in the evening, once I finally had some relief as I was able to watch mind-numbing television to take my mind off things, I received a text.

For privacy purposes, we will call the sender of the text Bailey. Bailey was and is a dear friend of mine who strayed off the Christian path a bit. She had cheated on her husband of just under two years, who was another dear friend of ours. Then, she decided to divorce her husband and live with the man with whom she cheated. We had had many discussions together on how what she was doing was wrong, but it didn't seem to matter. She texted me that night, asking me to remind her to tell me something when she called me the next day. My heart couldn't bear any surprises, so I guessed it. She was pregnant. I tried to keep my text supportive, but I was shaking. I ended the brief conversation that I would be praying for her, and that I loved her. Thankfully, it was revealed in a text. She likely would have been very hurt at my reaction. I wept, crying out, "Why her, Lord?! Why now?! How can she be blessed with such an incredible gift when I'm still grieving losing mine?!" I felt like the enemy had won. I couldn't take it anymore. The weight of the world was going to crush me, and only my mom and Chris could know why. *I had already given up my right to envy and jealousy, but this?!*

I called Bailey the next day and told her again that I would be praying for her, but I could not be involved in that aspect of her life yet. She said she understood, then told me the only time she'd contact me about her pregnancy was asking me if I wanted to be blocked when she posted online. I also referred her to the pregnancy center in our city as they offered free Christian counseling and other resources. I know it wasn't me who spoke when offering her the help of the pregnancy center because, after the fact, I was so upset that we would also be sharing the same counselor, but for opposite reasons; I would continue to see Debbie for healing from a miscarriage, while Bailey would see her for a healthy baby. *But maybe this would keep her from talking to me about being pregnant.* Painfully, but fortunately for me, God had other plans for our friendship.

All that next week, I kept feeling as though He wanted me to physically pray over Bailey and her baby. I argued, of course, because that was the last thing I wanted to do! I had spoken with some about my situation, who already knew about Bailey because she had revealed it to them, and the consensus was split 50/50. Half of the people with whom I had spoken encouraged me to pray over her, and half discouraged me from doing so as they knew my emotional stability was fragile, at best. I prayed all week, but I couldn't shake the idea of praying over her and her womb. Then, a friend came by to spend the night. (Again, for anonymity, we will call this friend, Lina). Lina was also friends with Bailey but, unlike me, she had been kept up to date on Bailey's prayer requests. Apparently, earlier in the week, Bailey had been bleeding quite heavily, so she and her boyfriend rushed to the hospital, preparing for the worst. Instead, they heard the baby's heartbeat, and received their first ultrasound along with the news that the baby was incredibly healthy. This news threatened to send me into a downward spiral as Bailey and her boyfriend had been given the very thing I desired most when in the hospital in Las Vegas. Don't get me wrong. I prayed for nothing but the best for her pregnancy, but I still hurt deeply thinking about it. Since then, she had other scares, but each time she was reassured that this baby was healthier than ever. If the thought of praying over her made me anxious before, it certainly became almost impossible to do now after hearing that news. Still, the thought persisted. I found out the news from Lina on Friday, and I was scheduled to meet Bailey after church on Sunday. I felt like I was kicking and screaming against God the entire time.

Sunday came all too quickly, and my heart was in my throat. Tears filled my eyes, and my mind flooded with thoughts of how to escape this task. I just couldn't do it. Then, during worship, the Lord took me on a journey through the story of the prodigal son found in Luke 15. Those familiar with the story know that in the story, the sinful son returns home to his father, only to find that his father openly embraces him and celebrates his safe return with a feast and other very important gifts. However, there is a lesser-known character in the story, the older brother. In this story, when the younger brother demands his inheritance, many gloss over the fact that the older brother also accepted his, instead of rejecting it or trying to talk to his younger brother, which culturally was considered just as sinful. At the end of the story, instead of celebrating that his brother had safely returned, he refuses to take his place at the feast and becomes angry with his father. He complains that he had never strayed from his father, yet he was never even given one young goat to have a feast with his friends. Then he says, "Yet, when this son of yours returns, after squandering your money on prostitutes, you *celebrate* by killing the fattened calf?!"

Here's the interesting, not-so-well-known fact: the older son already owned everything that was his father's. The eldest son of the time was given two-thirds of the inheritance, so if he wanted, he could have killed a goat or calf because it was already his. I used to really dislike the eldest son...until God showed me, he was who I was acting like with Bailey. In my mind and heart, I had done everything right. I was living my life serving Him, even participating in praying for healing, and awakening people to read God's Word with life among other things. I waited until marriage to be intimate, wrote a book to help others and myself heal, and stayed faithful to my husband. I didn't even accuse God of taking my baby when we lost her. However, during worship that morning, God replaced the eldest son's words with my own, "Yet when this daughter of yours returns after squandering your blessings, divorcing her husband, and sinning with her boyfriend, you *CELEBRATE* by giving her a *BABY*?!" Ouch. That hurt even typing it. As stated before, I was never angry with God for the fact that I lost my baby, but it turns out that I *was* angry with Him for blessing Bailey. After this conviction, I knew I didn't want to harden my heart, so I repented and asked His forgiveness. Then, I knew I had to pray over Bailey.

During the break, I told Bailey that after church I needed to pray over her, and then she told me she had felt like we needed to pray for healing over my life with our pastor. Almost as soon as we had both agreed to do this, a woman from that church walked up to me and handed me a support check for our next venture in missions. She stated compassionately that she was asking the Lord how much to give us monthly, and she heard, "Fifty dollars for Denelle, Fifty dollars for Chris, and Fifty dollars for their baby." I had been praying for our rainbow baby, so this little gesture meant the world to me and gave me hope that maybe the Lord intended us to have a healthy baby in the near future. The sermon ended too quickly. My heart could have ripped through my chest if it were beating just a little harder. Thankfully, Lina was also with us, so the three of us went to the parking lot to pray together. I told Bailey that I really didn't want to do this, but I needed to be obedient. Additionally, I didn't want to be envious of her anymore, and I wanted to be there for her. So, I prayed over her and over the precious little life forming in her womb. It wasn't eloquent or thought out at all; it was a simple, yet meaningful prayer. Then she and Lina prayed over me as well. When we had finished, none of our eyes were dry, and I received freedom from envy. I still knew that this baby had been conceived in sin, but he or she was a little blessing, a gift from our Heavenly Father to Bailey.

Since that time, Bailey and I have been able to speak about all aspects of her life, her prayer requests, and her future. During one of our in-person meetings, Bailey confessed all the sin she had committed since cheating on her husband and the excuses she had used to justify these sins. Then she proclaimed a sincere desire to get right with the Lord. She asked me to help her pray confession and repentance, so we did. It was absolutely incredible! At the time, I didn't know what the right and Godly thing for her to do was, but I knew that as long as she was seeking her Father's heart, He would lead her. Now, she continues to grow in her relationship with Jesus, her son, and the father of her child who became her husband. And all three of them are some of our dearest family friends now.

***

Bailey:

I had recently gotten a divorce from a great guy because of sin. I had faith in God but got distracted with temptation. When I separated from my husband, but my divorce was not final, I met this guy and started to date him. I felt bad but really liked the guy I met and wanted to start fresh. My divorce finalized, and I began to be more official in my new relationship by letting others know we were together.

Fast forward about a year and Denelle and I had grown closer as friends, and she really helped me grow closer to God. I couldn't forgive myself for the divorce and being the person I was being. I remember Denelle and I went to a park, and I was super vulnerable to her about my sin, and wanted to ask God for forgiveness, but didn't know how. She and I sat on the grass, bowed our heads and cried to God. I released all of my past self to try and move forward and make the best of the life God had given me.

I was growing closer and closer to God but had a big problem. I had been having premarital sex with my boyfriend but felt that I was too far into the relationship to stop. We were talking about marriage, and I was unsure what to do. One thing about me is that I have PCOS which makes it extremely hard to get pregnant. I thought that it was impossible at this point because I tried in my previous marriage and wasn't "not trying" in the current relationship I was in.

Denelle and I were fairly open with each other, and we both knew how much each other wanted a little one. I found out Denelle got pregnant, and I was extremely happy for her but still couldn't fight underlying feelings of jealousy. I tried to be there for her, but it hurt. Then, I found out the worst news…Denelle lost her precious baby in a miscarriage…all my feelings of jealousy went away, and I hurt for her. My heart wanted to give her the biggest hug and never let her go.

Denelle had become one of my closest friends and I never wanted her to feel this kind of pain, and then, I found out some life changing information. I was pregnant! *What?! Me?!* So many things were running through my head. *Am I going to be able to get through this pregnancy without issues from PCOS? Holy cow I'm pregnant? What am I gonna tell my family since we aren't married? Is God still going to love me? I need to get married! And...how do I tell Denelle after she just lost her baby?!* I didn't want Denelle to find out through social media or a mutual friend. I needed to tell her myself before anyone else found out.

Denelle was the second person I called after my mom, and I had no idea how to handle this conversation. Basically, I called her, told her, she cried and said congratulations, but there was no positivity in her voice. She sounded so hurt, and I didn't know what to say. I was told that she may not be able to be very present during my pregnancy. That hurt. A lot. But I understood.

We didn't talk much for what felt like weeks, and then God blessed me with a day that changed my life. Denelle reached out to me and told me she wanted to pray over my baby and me. Denelle and I went to church, and afterwards we went to the parking lot and met over by the cars. Denelle explained to me why she had not been talking to me much. She had felt like we were the brothers from the Bible where one had turned away from God, spent his money on the wrong things but eventually returned home. Their father celebrated the lost son, and it made the other son that was responsible feel really bad.

She had apologized because she knew I was trying to grow closer with God, and that conversation not only made me realize how much hurt I caused but how much God loved me and my baby. When she revealed her heart to me, I felt as though she, the older brother, was deciding to embrace my coming home.

Denelle became my best friend; I married the father of my child and we both follow the Lord to the best of our ability and continue to grow as a family. I am blessed to have my amazing family, and such a great friend.

After having my son, about a year later, I got pregnant a second time but was unaware of it. After approximately eleven weeks, my abdomen hurt really bad, and I felt like I needed to "push" like I did when I gave birth to my son. I gave birth to a small baby in the bathroom. I was in shock. Then I was hurt. Then I was in disbelief. Then I felt empty. My baby was not alive, and I was holding them in my hand. Lifeless. The worst feeling I had ever endured. *Is this what Denelle felt?* My heart was sore, my eyes were heavy, and my husband felt the exact same way.

I can't wait to one day meet my baby in heaven.

***

Chris:

Visiting my sister was one of the easiest parts of the journey for me. I was able to be around my family for the first time in a long time, since my family didn't live in our hometown and were not immediately available to visit whenever we returned home. Seeing my beautiful niece wasn't as heart rending for me as it was for Denelle. I got a glimpse of what Denelle would look like as a mother, and a part of who she was meant to be. I snuck a photo of the two of them together, but even without having to look at the photo, I can recall the image at any time. Denelle sat there with the small toddler in her lap in the middle of the playroom and the two looked beautiful together. Denelle didn't cry holding her niece like I thought she would. Instead, she embraced her and continued to read aloud to her as they shared that precious moment together. I remember feeling relieved that Denelle wasn't upset at being there, at least not outwardly.

During our stay, we made many new positive memories, and even got to share Word By Heart stories on the long car ride there. We went to the local taco shop, and just spent time reflecting on what God had been doing in our lives, and the ministry that he had given us. It was a nice break, until Denelle got that gut-punching text message from Bailey. I saw her returning smile fade and turn into anxiety and pain. She paced back and forth in the living room, hid away in my nephew's bedroom that we were staying in, and tried her best to still be a part of the time we had with our family. We argued quietly amongst ourselves on her speaking with Bailey for the time being. We had been there for Bailey and her husband while they went through their marital troubles and eventual divorce. This was the icing on the cake for me. Denelle needed to step away from her and the drama that followed so she could heal. Denelle, in her unlimited kindness, and gentleness, remained in contact with Bailey, who would later play a part in her healing. Bailey's child is now someone that Denelle and I both adore. Even through our pain that seems truly unbearable, God knows who he will use in our healing. The most unlikely person can be God's greatest source of restoration.

This time with my family was a pit stop along the long journey to recovery, even though at first, it looked like a setback.

Your turn: Who are you in the story of the Prodigal Son? Is there any resentment or envy trying to harden your heart? If so, what do you need to do to soften your heart once again?

9

My First Mother's Day

This is a day many mommies of children in Heaven dread because it is a day many truly feel invisible. Also, a day which is supposed to be filled with joy and appreciation of God giving women the blessing of a child is tinged with the grief of not being able to hold that little blessing. The entire day holds a trigger warning.

For me, the days leading up to Mother's Day were actually more difficult than the day itself. Starting a week before, I had received many emails daily about honoring moms, how you can treat yourself as a mom, etc. But the catch is that the subject in these emails were, of course, meant for moms with children on Earth. I allowed myself to read through some but deleted many (I knew I'd get similar ones the next Mother's Day). Friday, I asked for prayers from our Word by Heart class for all those in our class who were grieving, whether grieving our children, or our mothers. My intention was that we'd intercede right away, but the way I had phrased my request suggested that I wanted our Word by Heart family to simply cover us in prayers on their own time. It's important to note that at least four others were *also* grieving. Some, their mothers who had passed before, others, the hopes of being mothers as they were struggling with infertility, and then Chris and me. In my state of grief, I heard the lie of the enemy that I was indeed invisible, and that no one actually cared. I repented of the belief shortly afterward as God opened my eyes to ways that He showed He cared through others.

However, I was so upset after class for a whole slew of reasons, that I decided to eat lunch in the classroom alone, listening to and singing worship music, while everyone else ate in the dining hall as usual. It was then that the floodgates to my eyes burst open and poured out for over three hours. But the Lord also sent me His first gesture of love through one of our students, Karen, a long-time missionary to the nations, and a dear friend of mine. She simply listened to my apprehensions and declarations that I wasn't strong enough to endure this weekend. Then she gave me some suggestions of peaceful places to go on the actual day. Then she prayed fervently with me.

While she was doing this, my husband was tasked with going to the market to buy supplies for our mid-school celebration on Saturday. Little did I know, he was also plotting how to surprise me by speaking my love language, therefore honoring me on my first Mother's Day.

He knew that day and the days following were going to be very difficult for me, so while he was out, he purchased beautiful pearl earrings for me. I love pearls, especially the unique story of how they are formed, and thankfully, since we were on an island, there was such an abundance of them that they were inexpensive. He had also scoped out places in the mall we could go to enjoy Mother's Day together. He found a bookstore (a place in which we both could spend hours) and many other places; places to have delicious snacks, and places to allow me to purchase some gifts for myself. Truth be told, he had secretly been given money by family members to treat me, and to make my first Mother's Day special, regardless of the circumstances.

Saturday arrived, and with it, our school had a very exciting mid-school celebration with a picnic in the forest. We played games, laughed so hard our sides hurt, and ate delicious food, forgetting all the cares of the world. But that celebration ended much too quickly, meaning the dreaded Sunday was coming soon. While the rest of the school staff and students were returning to their homes, I still needed to buy flowers for our Mother's Day plan. Chris and I had decided to release flower petals into a nearby creek, each petal resembling a prayer or blessing that came from Sammy's short time with us. Knowing that others were also grieving for different reasons, we invited anyone to join us, and we would purchase a flower for them as well, but no one ever spoke up. So, I set out to buy two flowers, one for me, and one for Chris. Karen also needed to run some errands, so she graciously accompanied me, finding a taxi for us, and showing me the best place to buy a flower. I picked out two white roses, had them wrapped gingerly, then accompanied Karen in finishing the rest of her tasks. I was at peace that I had acquired the flowers, but my thoughts and feelings of isolation really threatened that peace. *No one really cares about the pain I am about to endure.*

Mother's Day arrived, and I would have to say that it was one of the hardest, yet most peaceful days I had experienced since my baby girl was born into Heaven. First, I Skyped my parents, who were also with other friends from church, and they prayed for me. When I emerged from the room, I was greeted by a chorus of our students, staff, and others from the base wishing me a happy Mother's Day. Then, it was time to prepare for our rose release. While we were praying, I began weeping too hard, and I was unable to bring myself to utter anything aloud. Unexpectedly, another voice from behind began praying for our healing, thanking God for bestowing the blessing of motherhood on me, and praying for our rainbow baby. To my surprise, our school leader, Lisbet, had shown up to our quiet ceremony, and started praying with us. She then picked her own little flower to release. All of this support happened within the first two hours of me being awake. To say I was overwhelmed is an understatement!

Then, we made our way to the creek. If there hadn't been water, I could have easily supplied it through my tears. Chris and I began taking turns, shakily peeling petal after petal off the roses, thanking God specifically for many aspects of giving us Sammy for a short time, and then for eternity in Heaven. As each petal floated down, I watched. *Where are these going to end up? Can Sammy see this? What is she doing right now?* Then, Lisbet prayed for healing over my womb and for our rainbow baby. She released the flower she had picked, then embraced me with a compassion that I know could have only come from our Heavenly Father.

After that, they flooded in. Message after message. Too many people to count had privately messaged me a happy Mother's Day, affirming that I *was* a mother, and that they were praying for me. Some had tagged me in posts about grieving mothers, recognizing the agony this day could bring, and some had shared my posts of being aware of "invisible" mothers. Thank goodness I had the foresight not to put on any makeup, because the entire day, tears streamed down my face. This time, they were warm tears of surprise and gratitude.

After I had been able to pull myself together decently enough, Chris hailed a taxi, and carried out phase two of his plan at the mall. We first entered the bookstore, and he turned me loose with the statement, "Choose anything you want." After browsing through the selections, I picked up one book, and said I was ready. He asked incredulously, "That's it?" Unwilling to believe *I* was only interested in one book, he instructed me to keep looking; so, I found another two, and stated, "That's it now." After leaving the store, he told me he wanted me to pick out another piece of jewelry made of pearl, so off to the jewelry shops we went. However, the selection had been quite picked through, and I personally preferred more simple items, so we left those shops empty-handed. But Chris wasn't finished yet. Then he took me into a couple of the other shops, though I only half-heartedly looked. Mother's Day sales were posted in each shop window, and there were children everywhere, so my eyes were very watery the entire time.

However, through blurred eyes, I did manage to find a sweet elephant pillow with a mother and baby, and a bouquet of fake flowers (real flowers don't stand a chance with me as their caregiver) for me and for a friend who had made the difficult decision long ago to choose life in an unexpected pregnancy, and then to give her daughter up for adoption into an incredibly loving family. It was heavy on my heart to honor her as well.

After that, Chris took me to eat some cheddar-flavored potato wedges, a favorite snack of mine when we made our way to this mall. As we were munching, we realized we had quite a long day already, so we decided to head home after one more shop.

We arrived just in time for the church session held at the base, but I wasn't sure I could attend. I had already been lovingly warned by members that mothers would indeed be honored, and the message would of course be on the topic of motherhood. What else can I expect on Mother's Day? Just because it was painful for me, it didn't mean that others couldn't or shouldn't be honored. However, for some strange reason, much like the previous nagging feelings I had had earlier on in the thick of my grief to approach the representatives from Pregnancy Care, I was *desperate* to attend the service. Chris was exhausted, and I think he secretly couldn't stand me being in pain, so he remained in the room, and I made my way slowly to the cafeteria where we held church.

We sang worship, heard a message on children and Hannah's story from the Bible, and then honored the mothers. The message was very applicable, and while I was listening through a small stream of tears, I felt the Lord speak to my spirit that Sammy's purpose was and is to honor God with her short life. After this, before anything else could happen, I had contemplated retreating to our room. I couldn't stand to face all the visible mothers being honored, while I stood silently pleading my case. Still my feet could not move. Inevitably, the time I was dreading the most came: the honoring of mothers. However, contrary to my fears, the church called up *all married* women and mothers; this included me!

Then, the kids of the church returned from Sunday School, bringing with them white roses and cards to give to their mothers. To my utter surprise, one of the little girls, not more than four years old, brought *me* a white rose, and the floodgates of my eyes burst once again. Then, as we were about to pray after all the mothers and married women had received their roses, another one of the little girls held two more roses. To my shock, she handed one to me, and one more to her mother. I tried to search for any other mother who did not yet hold a rose in her hand, but there were none. I graciously accepted, still wondering why I was chosen to receive two. All the church broke out into prayer over every woman standing at the front, and then I retreated to my room, too overwhelmed to speak.

That night, after I found the perfect place for my roses, Chris and I watched a movie, and as it finished, *he* began to weep. I was very confused, but he simply told me he had been receiving healing that day as well, and he felt like he could *finally* express what he was feeling because he saw that my heart was healing. We prayed, cried, and then peacefully drifted off to sleep.

Now, I have two children on Earth and two in Heaven, and my husband is always quick to include all my babies in some way on this special day of the year. One year, he personalized a book "from Hosanna, Sammy, and Micah." Another year, he wrote a beautiful poem from the perspective of Sammy and Micah. My favorite Mother's Day gift so far, though, was a Mommy-and-Me photo shoot with my two babies in my arms. However, when our photographer, April with Long-Lasting Photography, one of my dearest friends gave me my photos, including a photo book, she edited one of them to include shadows of children representing Sammy and Micah. She's done it for a couple more of my pictures since then, and each time, my reaction is the same: tears uncontrollably streaming down my cheek, my heart feeling as full as it can on this side of eternity.

***

Chris:

Mother's Day was quickly approaching, and I dreaded it for different reasons than Denelle. I feared she would be ignored or forgotten. I have never been more wrong about a group of people, not just the people of that country, but of the people with whom we lived. I spoke with a few people back home, asking them to remember Denelle on Mother's Day. Then I reminded them that the day would come early for us. I wanted to make sure she received happy wishes on the day and not the day after, when the US would be celebrating. I didn't see that anyone had read my request, so I worried that she would be looked over. One person in particular messaged me back and said something close to the sentiment that Denelle just needed to get over it, and that Jesus was coming back soon, so we shouldn't bring a kid into the world anyway. I was numb to their statement...*How could someone say something so heartless?!*

All I wanted was to see Denelle smile again. She had moments of joy or happiness but even the things that once made her happy, didn't draw a smile on her face. It was my mission to see her heart full, and not empty and longing on that day. Taking her to the mall was the only option that I knew of since we were relatively new to the country. I figured it had enough things to do to keep us occupied. In all honesty, I wanted to keep her away from the church service long enough for it to be over by the time we got back.

Once we did get back, and Denelle decided to go, I couldn't bring myself to join her. We had a good day so far, and I didn't want to see it ruined by her not being recognized by people we had *just met.* I couldn't go, not that it really mattered. Our bedroom door was mere feet away from the church service, and I heard it all. After a while, I did go outside and peer through the half-open blinds to the service. Peering in, I saw her, my beautiful wife, standing to one side of the line of women. Some women were gifted their flowers first, and I could tell she wholeheartedly didn't think she would receive one.

She graciously received a flower and was recognized as a mother. Nothing I could do on that day would come close to making her heart begin to heal as it began to in that moment. I then knew her healing was possible, and if so, then mine could begin also.

Denelle came back into the room a short time after and we exchanged the phrase of the day, "How are you doing? Are you ok?" After our check in with each other, we decided to watch a movie about a father who loses his daughter and comes to reconciliation with Jesus, himself. When the movie ended, we simply sat there in silence, just lying and holding each other. The credits rolled and so did the tears, for the both of us. I remember thinking that the movie wasn't *that* sad, and that I wasn't really *that* moved by it, but when the credits song came on, I simply couldn't hold in my pain anymore either, not from losing my child, and not from seeing my wife's hurt. We cried together while listening to the song *I'll Think About you* by The Messengers on repeat. On the anniversary of our children's eternal birthdays, we still listen to the song together, and the lyrics replay in my mind on a loop as we look back at this time of healing together.

Your Turn: Whether you have a child on Earth or in Heaven or both, you *are* a mama or daddy. How have you and others acknowledged that?

10

A Mother's Day Letter

Before I share this portion, I want to add a disclaimer that none of my family has attempted to communicate with anyone who has passed. That is not something in which we believe. When my mom wrote that she heard what my sweet baby wanted to tell me, it was simply something in her heart. I do not now, nor will I *ever* endorse communication with those on the other side of eternity.

This letter appeared in my inbox that day from my own mother, and I have debated between treasuring it personally in my heart or sharing it for others to read in their child's stead.

"My dear sweet daughter, I so badly want to send you something for Mother's Day. I wanted to paint you a beautiful picture: elephants, a big bouquet of flowers, an inspirational saying. I even thought about sending you a card or even a real bouquet of flowers, perhaps lilies. But I didn't do any of this. Why? Well, mainly because I don't have an address to send any of these to. HAHAHAHAHA! So, what I have decided to give you is a letter from Sammy. This is what I hear that sweet baby wanting to tell you:

'*Dear Mommy,*

I see your beautiful, sweet face and simply want to hug you and squeeze your cheeks. I'd love to give you a big kiss right on your rosy cheek. And one day I will do all of this! One day I will run into your arms and giggle, squeal and tell you all kinds of stories about my adventures in Heaven. For now, please be comforted in knowing that Jesus is awesome. He plays with me, He loves me, and He cares for me. He is taking great care of me until I can meet you face to face. Jesus loves me and all the children! Mommy, you are a wonderful Mommy. I know that you loved me at the moment you even decided you wanted to have children. You loved me even more when you found out that I was developing in your womb. You loved me even more when you found out I was in Heaven. And you love me more each and every day. I love you too Mommy. I look forward to meeting you face to face one day. Until then, please dry your tears and let your heart heal. I love playing up here with Jesus and Joey and all the other kids. Let your heart heal so that your body, mind, and soul can heal as well. You need to be healthy so that you can play with my soon to be earthly siblings. Give my daddy a big hug and tell him I love him too and I look forward to running through a great big heavenly meadow with him and giggling and jumping around. Happy Mother's Day to my beautiful Mommy. Love you to the Heavens and back.

Love Always,

Sammy'"

I encourage you to reread this letter, but in place of Sammy's name, insert your baby in Heaven's name or nickname.

11

Micah's Story

Micah was supposed to be our rainbow baby, the return of my joy, the final part to my healing. He was supposed to be the "rainbow of hope after the storms of grief" caused by miscarriage...Or so we thought... Just before we left for the Philippines, Chris and I made it very publicly known that we were praying and trying for a rainbow baby. It was no different when we arrived in the Philippines. Every chance we got, I asked for prayers for our rainbow baby. At the time, I was not as emotionally stable as I had thought, and I falsely believed that a rainbow baby would bring my healing. *After all, I wasn't going to lose this next one, right?* I am embarrassed to admit that having a rainbow baby became my heart's desire over all else, and I was obsessed. The idea likely would have become an idol if it had not already become one.

Each month, as Aunt Flow appeared, though, I relived losing my baby once again, and my hopes of a rainbow kept drifting further and further away. That, coupled with the fact that there was a giddy little family with a newborn baby on the base, threatened to overtake me. This little baby boy was so adorable, which made things worse for me. My arms still physically ached to hold my baby, so one day, I decided to try to hold the little newborn. *Perhaps that would help the ache in my arms and in my heart.* Wrong. The encounter only ended with me quickly and clumsily giving him back to his mother, then racing out the door to my room the rest of the night to sob. It seemed that holding a baby in my arms only continued to break my heart and cause my arms to ache even more for my own.

To top it off, each week more and more of my friends announced their pregnancies, including one friend who hadn't even been married for half a year. Thankfully, this time, envy remained silent, but impatience and hopelessness began to creep their way into my heart. I cried for hours after finding out about that particular friend, wondering how many pregnant women I'd pray for before I could join that list...or *if* I would ever join that list. In hindsight, it honestly didn't take us long when we *had* been actively trying by tracking my cycle, but though it was only a few months, it felt like an absolute eternity.

The students and staff in the Philippines were continuously so gracious to me, and they agreed to pray for these things with us. Weekly, new people approached us, telling us that during their prayer times, they received a verse or an image encouraging us that the time of hope would be soon. In addition to all of that, Chris and I had been having many dreams of our rainbow, and I had felt an overwhelming sense that by Mother's Day I would be expecting again. Unfortunately, I wouldn't know until a week after Mother's Day, but it was indeed true!

On the morning of May 23rd, I gazed at the two pink lines I had been so desiring to see! Just like that, I became a mother of two! We were elated, so we video chatted with my parents that same morning, and joined worship that night *filled* with joy! I decided to try to hold the newborn again, and I was so successful that my smile was beaming from ear to ear! This time, my weeping was filled with happy tears. The next day, we told our students and staff during our weekly reflections. Everyone was ecstatic, and joyfully prayed over Baby Scanlan and me! I was flooded with gratitude as I began to truly have hope that this baby would be the one to fill my empty arms. Then, on Sunday, the spotting started. At first, it was pink, but all too quickly, it became the crimson red of which I was so petrified. Chris and I rushed to the hospital, and our school leader, Lisbet, accompanied us. By the time the doctor was able to see me, I was bleeding heavily and dreaded the worst. I was taken for an ultrasound, but even with a healthy baby, our little one was much too little to be detected. The only good sign was that my uterine lining was still thick like it was supposed to be at that possible gestation. We were told we'd have to schedule a follow-up appointment for that Friday, or sooner if I was still bleeding.

One malicious lie with which I had secretly struggled when Sammy went to Heaven was that my faith wasn't enough to save Sammy. It plagued me daily. The enemy taunted me with the thought day and night. *Had I truly believed in the impossible, maybe God might have chosen to save my baby. Had I rebuked the enemy more strongly...Had I done this, this, or this more...* While I know these thoughts are not true, they are all too common for the many families who share our pain. After some praying and talking together, Chris helped me to find the strength to fight for this one. I was put on bedrest the entire week, so it allotted me much time to pray, worship, read my Bible, and read inspirational books. In addition, all the class was praying, while Chris was fasting dinners for this child. It was the longest week of my life, or so I thought, until Wednesday finally came. Chris and I and all the staff and students were positive we would see the miracle that we had hoped for with Sammy. This little rainbow would be completely okay.

I had scheduled an appointment with a high-risk OBGYN, and I was encouraged when her office was decorated with Scripture. That encouragement was swiftly trampled, though, when she conducted the ultrasound. At that time, I was still bleeding, but Sunday night was the only night I had passed small clots. She told me my lining was much thinner than the ultrasound taken at the hospital, and that she wanted me to get a blood test to see if I had had an ectopic pregnancy or not. But as far as a baby, she saw nothing, and told me that miscarriages are common, and it's possible I wasn't even pregnant to begin with. However, I pulled out my very positive tests from multiple days of testing, and she concluded that I was probably miscarrying. She planned to check my blood test on Friday before making anything final. I returned back to the base again, devastated, but many still felt very positive about this baby. Everyone with whom we lived believed in the power of prayer. Anything was possible if it was God's will. So, we prayed. This time, I felt like I was supposed to ask our doctor for just one more week. Additionally, I had been hearing the words in my heart, "It is not time to grieve," over and over again throughout that week. While hearing this, I kept asking God to confirm it through another person, but never told anyone, including my husband, because I wanted it to come directly from the Lord. So, Chris and I went to my appointment with confidence; but the HCG results showed I had lost my pregnancy.

My hope was yet again restored when the doctor looked at the test results, yet still decided without my prompting, that we would wait another week before determining the final results. On the car ride home, without having prior knowledge of the words upon my heart, Karen uttered my confirmation, "It's not time to grieve." Despite the circumstances, she had confirmed what I had been hearing, and the doctor decided to give us another week! So, we waited, again, for the longest week of my life. Chris and I worshiped, prayed, read our Bibles, and spent much intimate time with God as I was still practically on bed rest. Thursday night was our scheduled weekly worship with the base church, and I felt compelled to share the hope within my heart, but then I ended our story and prayer with, "But even if He doesn't heal this baby, and we don't see our miracle, God is still good." And I meant it. It was one of the most painful statements I have ever made as I realized that maybe it was not His will for this miracle to happen either. I swallowed hard, trying to grasp whatever hope remained. It was truly a Shadrach, Meshach and Abednego faith moment, just without the threat of being incinerated (starts in Daniel 3). That night I wrote out my prayer not knowing that it was not a prayer for Micah, but for the babies to come.

Abba,

You have blessed Chris and me with so much. You have made us parents by giving us sweet little Sammy, even if for just a short time. You have protected her from harm and suffering, and she lives daily in your presence, worshiping you. Thank you that we have hope of seeing her, and we will live together as one family in your Holy presence. Thank you that you have collected my tears and are healing my heart. Thank you that you have given us new life growing within my womb and that you have provided such faithful people to hold up my hands and Chris' hands in worship and prayer to you, the Author of Life. Nothing is too big for you. If you are willing, you can stop the bleeding and help this little baby grow within my womb. As I don't know how the breath of life enters the baby within my womb, I don't understand the ways of you, Lord. But I love you and I trust you. Thank you for this miracle child and for wiping away my tears. I have heard you whisper that now is not the time to grieve. That you are God, and you have promised this sweet child to us. Send your angels to protect the three of us. You are holy, and good. You fight when we are weak, and you alone are our strength. You have blessed us with another child, another arrow in our family quiver. Show your handiwork when we go to the doctor. Show your miraculous nature, and answer the prayers of all of us, Holy Father. We trust you and leave this situation in your hands. I will keep my eyes on you, Jesus, as you lead me out onto the water. I know you love us, and I know you are for us. Give joy back to my heart. Replace the fear, except of reverence of you, with your joy in your Holy Presence. Fill this place with you, and your truth. Increase all of our strength as we pray for this child, and as we see you answer our prayers. Let the healthy birth

> *of this child be one to give many hope because you hear the cries of our hearts. You are good, and we don't deserve your mercy which you so freely give to us. Show us your glory in all circumstances. Renew our faith and the authority to stand.*

Friday finally arrived, and I was 98% positive we would all be surprised by a thick lining, and a small baby. I walked in confidently with a smile on my face, and a heart light as air, practicing how I would explain that I serve a God of miracles. We were about to see a *true* one. I envisioned the look on the doctor's face as we watched the little ultrasound together. But...that never materialized. Instead, my doctor informed me that everything had cleared out, and my cycle seemed to have started over again as if nothing had ever happened. But it did. In those two weeks, I experienced a lifetime with this precious baby, and with the Lord. I was reassured I would be ovulating in about a week if I wanted to try again. To say I was crushed is definitely an understatement. And this time, I felt my faith was going to be really shaken. Why had we received all these confirmations, signs, and insurmountable peace, yet this was our result?! *Why hadn't we been saved by the fire? We did all the things. Chris fasted, we used Jesus' name in full faith of this miracle, anointed my belly many times with oil, we shared our story with any who had ears to hear, and made promises to share this baby's miracle story with the world.* But God still said, "No."

I also began to struggle with the idea that I may never have and maintain a healthy pregnancy. *Maybe it wasn't God's will that we have living children on Earth.* I'd hoped that wasn't true, but could I really know for sure? I didn't know how many more times I could lose a baby and survive. However, one thing stood out immediately; this time, no one could accuse me of not having enough faith to save my baby. That lie was finally quenched. But that's the thing, it was never on me. The fasting, worship, and everything else we had done was never truly about the baby or me. It was about coming to a deeper place of intimacy with God together as a family, and that's exactly what happened. I had come to the true Shadrach, Meshach, and Abednego moment in my faith simply because the Lord led Chris and me into a deeper dependence and love with Him, whether He gave us the miracle or not.

After informing everyone on base, and spending Saturday in my Bible, listening to worship music, and doing a lot of crying again, I was still so in love with Jesus. The words I was prompted to share Thursday night clanged like a gong in my heart. Even though He didn't, He was still good and still God. Of course, I was hurt and confused, I still am, but didn't want to give up. In prayer, we felt this one was a boy, and we named him Micah, meaning, "Who is like the Lord?" In the midst of this whirlwind of emotions, God seemed to show me His heart for me, and to give me hope.

While worshiping in solitude, a visitor to our base, a veteran to missions in the Philippines approached me boldly and said he felt he should pray over me-specifically my womb. He had prayed over many before, and had seen an abundance of beautiful answers, so he wanted to do so for me. The funny thing is that just before he made his way over, I had been asking God *if* He desired to give us a baby to hold and care for on Earth. My prayer moments before the missionary approached was similar to the one I prayed about a future husband prior to meeting Chris. "If you don't want me to have a baby to hold in my arms, please take this painful desire away, and show me what to do instead."

Monday morning, a student pulled me aside and stated that she had been praying for me. She felt to tell me that it is not a time to grieve, because God has both my beautiful babies in Heaven, safe in His arms. Again, like Karen, this student did not know that this statement was a huge confirmation to me. Then I realized that even though the loss was still so fresh, none of the healing in my heart that God had done after Sammy went to Heaven was lost after Micah went to Heaven. Envy and Jealousy were still silenced, and I felt even more of an urgency to pray for my pregnant friends, desperate for none of them to know this pain. Depression and despair visited less frequently, and were much weaker than before, and I wondered: *could I still hold that newborn baby and keep it together?* Shortly after that, I discovered the answer was a resounding, "Yes!"

Despite all the progress in healing, the pain of our hearts breaking again was enough for both Chris and me to decide not to actively try again for a while. We would take things slowly again, and I would not be tracking my ovulation, or stressing over tracking anything else I had been doing when trying to conceive Micah. My rainbow and return of my joy was from God and God alone. Of course, there were still triggers, but I turned to God when I came across them. Aunt Flow's visits were still flashbacks now to both of the lowest points in my life, but somehow, I was less emotional. However, grief is not linear; it simply hits at the most random moments, and sometimes depression just sets in.

One of those times was after our school in the Philippines when Chris and I went to Cambodia to staff at that Word by Heart school. It was directly after graduation in the Philippines that we went, but we were excited for a new adventure and to see some old friends we had met in Las Montañas. Shortly after arriving, a member of the church on the campus we were staying died suddenly, and it was as if the entire campus was filled with grief. Anyone who had ever lost someone seemed to be experiencing the depression stages again, and unfortunately Chris and I were not excluded. My bout of depression had begun two weeks before we left the Philippines, then it had let up when we arrived in Cambodia, masked by the excitement of a whole new experience in a new country. Yet it returned strongly that particular week. I just wanted to stay in our room and cry. How I wished we could wake from this nightmare. However, after the week was up, the grief had lifted almost as quickly as it came on, and so did my spirits.

***

Chris:

Throughout our first three months in the Philippines, we received healing and, of course, the loss you just read about. Denelle and I had moments of questioning our faith, but never moments of doubting God. We knew Jesus was still faithful and it was during this time that I believe Denelle and I grew closer together. We prayed more together, read scripture daily, began learning new Word by Heart stories, and had small Saturday dates at a restaurant across the open airport runway. It was during that time that we dug deeper into God's word together and separately. Micah 7:7-8 stuck out to us one night during this loss, hence the name we chose. "As for me, I look to the Lord to help. I wait confidently for God to save me, and my God will certainly hear me. Do not gloat over me, my enemies! For though I fall, I will rise again. Though I sit in darkness, the Lord will be my light." The name would be a source of comfort over the next several months as we continued to pray together, and ultimately came to a place of giving up trying to have a baby and deciding to place it all into the Lord's hands. After all, who is like the Lord?

As we looked to the Lord for help, we became more efficient in our duties to help run the school that we were staffing. For some time, I believe we were more burdensome to our great leaders. Their unwavering patience with us was purely of the Lord. We had coffee meetings to see how we were doing, flower ceremonies, companionship on our journey to get news from the doctors, good or bad. The support we received was truly divine and inspiring. With a new resolve to place things into Jesus' hands, I felt more prepared to do the tasks that he had entrusted me with; cleaning duties, playing drums for community worship, teaching in class, etc. I felt a new sense of purpose and understanding in that time of reading God's word. We would share our almost daily relations with each other and the Jesus of the Bible, became evermore, the Jesus of our hearts.

Having gone through everything that you have read thus far, we resolved to give up ourselves and our desires, and waited for the Lord to grant us the true desires of our hearts, which was to serve Him. Anything else was a pure blessing. After all, who is like the Lord?

In the beginning, when we lost Sammy, the hardest part for me was being there for Denelle and trying not to be angry. Not at her and not at God, just at the situation. As time passed, we met with friends and church family. I began to become more and more angry, and this time, with God. We couldn't touch the hem of His robe. Who would carry our mats? Who would take us into the pool as the water stirred? We prayed so hard, and believed in a miracle that never came. My mountain was unmoved. My tree remained planted. No one came to him to beg for our case. No healing power left Him. Or at least that's how I felt.

I still loved the Lord and tried to push past the angry thoughts. I felt that they were just the enemy trying to make me bitter. I tried to dive myself into God's word and learn more Bible stories for Word by Heart. I remained by Denelles' side as she cried, and laughed, and processed everything. I never processed. I was angry. How many times had I prayed for her healing? How many times had I prayed for her to have some relief? *Are you even listening anymore?!* Feeling as if the Lord was not, like a child, I stopped talking to him. I still wanted to restore my relationship with Jesus and with that in mind, we left for Cambodia.

I had been there with Denelle through everything that she has shared with you, but never felt I had a role. *How could I help her?* I felt I had no help and could do nothing but be by her side. Even when I mentioned my struggles to others, I was only met with platitudes. "The Lord works in mysterious ways," or "The teacher is always silent during a test." These phrases are not helpful, and people sound stupid saying them. *Please just stop!* I would think in those moments.

I hadn't been struggling with where I should open my next mega church. I lost my child and my Papa, who could have helped me, didn't. Or at least that's how I felt. I stepped out of the boat, and He was going to let me drown.

While we were in the Philippines we lost our second baby, Micah. All I could do was read God's Word and press into Him. I learned more about Jesus in a week's time than I had the last six years of being a Christian. I didn't want to be angry, but I was, and I knew He wasn't afraid of my anger.

One day, I don't remember when, He showed me what I had missed. I saw a desert road that angled downward. The road was dusty and full of jagged rocks. I was running barefoot, as fast as I could, down it. We all know that feeling as a kid, running so fast that we feel weightless and like we can't stop. All I could see was Jesus at the end of the road.

He was yelling, "Come to me! Run! I won't stop you! I'm always here! Run to me!" I cried out in reply, "I'm coming! Please don't leave! I'm coming Papa!" He continued calling to me, "I'm right here! I'll catch you!" At this point, He was almost kneeling, arms outstretched, simply waiting for me. I wept, "I'm sorry! Please, catch me!" Then, in an instant, I hit His chest. It was not a hard crash. It didn't hurt, but it was firm. All I could see was me as a little boy clinging to my Jesus, my friend, my love. I was crying, and all I could do was be embraced. *Where are they? Why couldn't we keep them?* All I heard was, "In my Father's house, there are many mansions. If it weren't so, I wouldn't have told you. Look, I've prepared a place for them."

Then, it was bright, and I was standing on a pathway. My heart was beating through my chest. There were tall buildings all around that were glittering like gold, and then I knew where they were. I ran. He wasn't with me, but I could feel His presence all around. "Keep going! You'll find them. You know where they are." I reached a room with a simple wooden door and opened it. I looked around and saw it; a bed in the corner, with a crib next to it. Children's toys were scattered, and yet in their own place. I saw a sun and a rainbow mural on the wall. *This was their room.* In an instant, I saw her: a small blonde girl with pigtails holding a small boy in a swaddle. She didn't say anything, but she smiled. She knew who I was. She didn't say it, but I could tell she was expecting to see me. My heart was still pounding. I don't remember if we embraced. If we did, I didn't see it. But I did *feel* it. I couldn't help but cry, and then again in a moment, Jesus had them both in His arms. All he said, with loving tears in His eyes too, was, "Hosanna is coming." And then it was over.

Your Turn: Take time to read the story of Shadrach, Meshach, and Abednego in Daniel 3. Have you come to a faith strong enough to say, "But even if you don't..." or are you still struggling? Give it to God.

Part III- Letters to Our Babies in Heaven

12

Letters to Heaven

I want to take a minute to acknowledge all the moms and dads with babies in Heaven. You are seen, and you are loved. Please use the words of some parents from all different faith and spiritual backgrounds to their children to bring comfort to your hearts. You may disagree, and that's okay. These parents poured their hearts out so that you could be encouraged to do the same. After reading, use the space provided to write out a letter to your baby/babies born into heaven. I understand that this is likely the most painful part of this book, but also can be one of the most impactful. Take your time and give yourself grace as you complete this. You will likely be opening up old wounds that have never healed properly either from trying to move on from the pain, or possibly some wounds that were only ever covered as you try to stuff your feelings down because "No one ever talks about it."

Dear Baby Sammy,

I've loved you since the moment your mommy told me that you would be joining our family! I'm sorry we don't get to meet but I swear I know your face and your sweet voice. I can see your golden hair and brown eyes. I can feel your tiny hand in mine. I can feel the way you would look at me as your daddy. I can see your mansion in paradise and how you're not alone. Thank you for sharing your room with your little brother Micah. I can see your perfect smile and hear your infectious laugh. I know you without having known you and I'll love you forever!

Dear Little Man,

Micah, I love you to heaven and back! You're such a strong little guy! Thank you for bringing your mother and I such joy and giving us strength. Like your sister, I can see your face and your smile! I can see the joy you bring to others, and I can feel your embrace even though we are apart. I can feel your hand in mine as well and can feel your little body as if you're sitting on my lap and letting me hold you close! I can see you playing and enjoying your time in heaven with all the other little kids. I pray you always know we love you and when I arrive, you and your sister meet me at the gates!

Love,

Daddy

***

My Sweet Sammy and Mighty Micah,

I hope Jesus reads this to you. If love could have been enough to keep you with me on this side of eternity, just one thought would have done it. I miss you every day of my life, and I know that even with the many blessings Jesus has in store for my family, I will have to wait a little while longer until I can see two of my greatest blessings. I pray often that the Lord would give me a glimpse of your faces and let me hear just a bit of your beautiful laughter. I wonder, which one of you looks like Daddy, if either of you do? Your brother and sister here look like me mainly, but they have Daddy's toes. Do you? Do you have blonde hair like them? When I meet you on that beautiful day,

I know my heart will recognize you. And you better get ready for the biggest hug.

I do have peace in the fact that you never knew pain, or sickness, never experienced bullying, splinters, or fear. You were born into perfect love. Don't worry. Everyone who meets me knows about you and the deep footprints you have left on my heart. You have changed my life for the better, and even though my time carrying you was much too short, and ended in quite a lot of pain, if I were given a chance, I'd choose that time with you over again. Everyone knows that I have two beautiful babies in Heaven, and two on Earth. I hope I can be the mommy to you and to your siblings on Earth that would make you proud. God has used you to heal so much of me, and ultimately to bring Him even closer to *my* heart. He has used our story to help bring healing to so many other parents whose babies you get to play with in Heaven. I am so blessed to have been able to carry you for the time I did. But I cannot wait until the day that I can embrace you in my arms! Until then, I'll continue to carry you in my heart.

I love you both to Heaven and back!

Love,

Mommy

***

Dear Sammy and Micah,

I love you and miss you! I feel sad when I can't be with you, but I can't wait to see Jesus together with you in Heaven.

Love,

Sissy

***

Dear Baby F,

I remember you most around Christmas, as this was, when you were due to enter our lives. We had dreamed about you, since the moment that we had met each other, and you were wanted and loved from the day that we knew you were going to join us. But shortly after twelve weeks, we were notified that you were no longer alive, and the role of future mother and father ceased to exist. I was so sad that I was never going to meet you. I was so sad that you were never going to feel how much we loved you. But shortly after that, I got pregnant with another baby. And throughout that whole pregnancy, I was afraid until Carolyn was born. And after I had Carolyn, I felt guilt, guilt for loving a baby that was not you. Then I realized that I needed to thank you. I had to thank you, because we realized that for some reason, Carolyn was the baby that we were supposed to have. She was the person that was supposed to complete our family, and you must have known that. You must've known that for some reason, you needed to sacrifice yourself, so that Carolyn could join our family. We realized that if we would've had you, we never would've met Carolyn. So, thank you, Baby F, for doing what you knew you needed to do so that our family could be complete. And I know that wherever you are, you're with my mom, and you are loved beyond imagination because being a grandma was her most favorite thing. I often wonder who you would be today, how many lives you would have affected in your life, but I know that you gave so we could have Carolyn. Thank you.

Much love,
Mom and Dad

***

Genesis,

Your mom and I love you so much, even though we never got to meet you. Our short time together brought us so much joy that you would soon be a part of our family and you will forever have a place in our hearts. We will always miss you here but are comforted by knowing we will one day be able to finally meet you in heaven. Until that day comes, just know we will never forget about you and pray you are always with us in spirit.

With much love,
Daddy-Chris W.

***

Dear little one in heaven,

The first thing I want to tell you is that you are loved and wanted. Even though you were only here for nine short weeks, we had already told our friends the happy news and bought things for you. We still have the Mickey Mouse blanket that we bought, and I want you to know that your two younger siblings have been wrapped in it and have lain on it to play.

The second thing I would tell you is that we mourned you. Life did not just move on. You are remembered. I don't know if God allows you to look down from heaven and see us. But please know that your sisters remember you. When we draw a picture of our family, they always remind me to add a little baby with angel wings in the picture. When asked how many are in our family, they talk about you. "I have two sisters and one brother in heaven." They will always say.

Your life here on earth was short, but it left a mark, and your absence is felt.

The day you left us God told me, "When you walk through the waters, you will not be swept away." He knew a flood of grief was coming, but he wouldn't let it overcome. It took a long time, but the grief has been overshadowed by joy: Joy that you lived and that we said "yes" to steward your little life. Joy because when your little heart stopped beating here, you woke up in heaven. The first face you saw was Jesus. Your nannies were the angels. You never again knew pain or sadness. You got to be raised in heaven.

And the grief was swallowed up by the joy of knowing that the day we arrive in heaven will be the best day ever, because our family will finally be complete.

I don't question God's wisdom anymore in taking you before I was ready. But I do ask Him to tell you things. I ask Him to tell you that we love you. That you have a mom and dad and siblings who miss you. That you aren't alone. And I ask Him to tell you to pray for your siblings. This world down here can be really hard and painful, and some days have more tears than others. So, I ask Him to let you pray for us with heaven's perspective, which we need so desperately some days.

So, until we all meet again up there, know that you are deeply loved, and we can't wait to get to know you.

***

Dear Baby of Mine,

I did not give you a regular name per se. I've always called you; Dear One, My Baby, and Dear Baby of Mine. Back when I lost you, it wasn't as common to give the babies lost early in pregnancy names. I don't know why, I mean you are still my baby, I still count you as one of my babies, so why not a name? It also wasn't very common back then to even talk a lot about having had a miscarriage unless it was in a medical setting.

Looking back to that time of my life when I lost you, I know that I wasn't doing things the best way at the time. But I also thought that everything was pretty cool at the time. Then things changed. They changed drastically. How and when I lost you was horrible, beyond believable even to myself sometimes. The horrible act of another person made me lose the one thing that I had always wanted my entire life.

My whole life all I wanted was to be a mom, to have kids, lots of kids, and be a mom. I didn't care how I got kids, gave birth to, adopted, step, fostered, whatever. I just wanted to be a mom. Being a veterinarian or a sign language interpreter or a teacher always came after being a mom. So, to know that I was pregnant, and my dreams were beginning to come true was the most beautiful, amazing thing ever! Maybe not the way I had imagined it happening, but I was becoming a mom. Then in one moment and the horrible act of another, you were gone.

My hopes, my dreams, my life as I knew it ended that day. Even though losing you just about killed me, it also woke me up. The life I was living was not the life I knew that God wanted for me. So, you being here growing inside me was my dream but losing you saved my life and that of your twin brother. You see, when I lost you, I didn't know that there were two. Two babies growing inside of me. Two babies of my dreams. But not knowing that allowed me to leave the life I was in after I lost you. I left as soon as I possibly could. I called my parents, I apologized, and I asked to come home. Without skipping a beat, they were right there to help me pack up my things, to keep me safe once more.

You, Dear Baby of Mine, in losing your life saved mine, saved your twin brothers, brought me and your grandparents back together, and I believe saved their lives also. Within the first year of your brother's life, my dad had to have open heart surgery, your brother was his rehab partner, I took care of my dad during this time, took him to all appointments and everything while my mom had to work full time. Shortly after my dad was back to work full time, my mom fell on the ice on our driveway and almost severed part of her leg, ankle and foot. I found her, brought her in the house and helped my dad get her to the hospital. She had to be transferred to a bigger, better hospital than what we had, requiring multiple surgeries and weeks in the hospital. When she came home, I took care of her, taking her to all of her appointments and such for over nine months of recovery and rehab, while my dad was back to work full time.

I was there to help them both because of you. So, you see, Dear Baby of Mine, you saved so many lives in your far too short life. You were and still are mine. I wanted you even before I knew I was pregnant with you. You, my little Miracle, are one of the best things that ever happened to me. I know now that those two wonderful parents of mine that brought me back home and took care of me and then I in-turn took care of, are with you now, enjoying all the love from you. For seventeen years, you've had your PaPa with you and for the last four-and-a-half years, you've had your Nannie with you. It's been thirty-one years since you saved my life and your twin brother's life.

I was nineteen when I got pregnant and lost you. I was barely two months into being twenty when your twin brother was born a month early. Finding out that I was still pregnant but had lost one baby of two was strange. I mean I was thrilled at still getting to have a baby, but I also had still lost a baby.

Not many people knew that I had lost a baby. I'm from a very small town in Illinois with a bunch of small towns not too far away. We lived in one town, went to school in the next one over and went to church in the next one over from there. So, everyone knew everyone and everything about everyone. So, for not many people knowing that I had lost one baby was really strange. So, I just didn't talk about you much. Not because I was ashamed or that I didn't love you, that couldn't be farther from the truth. It just wasn't done much back then.

I had known most of my life that my mom had suffered a miscarriage before I was born but after losing you, she and I really talked about what it was like for us both to lose a child, and we became closer because of it.

I want you to know that I long for the day I can actually hold you in my arms. Oh, what a day that will be. Having lost you so early on I never got to see you or hold you. I could only dream. I've missed you for thirty-one long years.

I mentioned that you saved my life and your brother's and grandparents lives but in writing this to you now, I realize you saved so many more lives than that. Because of you, I have seven more children. Four of whom would not be here if not for you. Three are my 'step-kids', which, we don't say it that way; they are all our kids. His, mine and ours. I have eight grandchildren so far. I have a man who loves me the way God intended, who has told me that he wouldn't be here if not for me. So once again, because of you, so many lives were saved.

My Dear Baby of Mine, in rereading what I have written here, I realized that I had actually given you a name. Miracle. Miracle you were, and Miracle you shall forever be. My Baby-Miracle. I Love You.

Love, Your Mommy- Tarina Kasputis

Your Turn: Write your own letter to your baby/babies in Heaven:

Author's Note Cont'd

It is at this point in the story that I must stop and warn you, my readers. Some of your hearts are still yearning for that baby to hold in your arms. I share this next part as this is a piece of my family's story of hope and restoration. However, I make no false promises that this will be how everyone's story will unfold. Some of you, and I admit I don't understand why, will be told, "No," even more times than I, and might never experience the rainbow of hope in the same way. I encourage you to seek the Lord in all things. A reason to praise Him, to shout "Hosanna! Praise the Lord!" *is* coming. But it might not be in the same way or timeframe as my story. Let me assure you, if you haven't already deduced, I am *not* more deserving than others of this miracle. My faith is *not* more than yours. That is *not* why my prayers were answered in the way I desired. I didn't say or do all the right things. I didn't follow a certain formula. God just said, "Yes!" I will never understand why, but then again, who wants to worship a God who can fully be understood?

As we proceed forward in this journey together, two key terms I will use are: rainbow baby, and pot of gold. A "rainbow baby" is a baby born after a miscarriage, or in my case, miscarriages. Then, a "pot of gold baby" is also sometimes called a "double rainbow," and is a baby born after the rainbow baby.

Your Turn: What is your reason to praise Him?

Part IV - Hope Restored

"For there is hope for a tree. If it is cut down, that it will sprout again, and that its tender shoots will not cease."
(Job 14:7 NKJV)

13

Hosanna is Coming!

While still in Cambodia, shortly after that week of grief, Aunt Flow was late again. In disbelief, I held that little test showing two pink lines once again. My third pregnancy! My heart yearned desperately for this one to last. We hadn't even been trying. It just happened, and so soon after Micah was born into Heaven. I fought hard to keep my hope. Again, after two losses, the fear crept in. *How could I move forward if this one didn't make it into my arms as well?* But still I fought. I fought to be joyful, filled with hope, dreaming about the growing baby bump, the tiny kicks, and everything to come after that. I fought because I wanted this pregnancy to be marked with insurmountable joy, not fear and anxiety. I called my parents to video chat, and my mom remarked that I looked kind of sad. I replied, "That's strange. I thought I was glowing." Catching on immediately, my parents once again rejoiced, and the joy over this little baby filled all of our hearts.

At our staff meeting, Chris and I relayed the good news to our fellow staff members-several of whom had been part of the journey since the beginning in Las Montañas. Then, that Friday during our fun day, Chris and I shared both the beautiful news and the prayer request for our hearts and this baby with our students. Unfortunately, we hadn't even been able to reveal to anyone on the base yet, when later the following week, that familiar warm trickle sent terror and dread into my heart. Over the weekend, I had become desperately ill with food poisoning. The symptoms continued to last for over a week, and they were very obviously not due to my being pregnant. However, in addition to the food poisoning, I began to experience the pregnancy complications, invoking terror that we'd have to face yet another loss.

Chris and I raced to the hospital due to these complications with one of our Khmer friends to translate when this baby was a little over six weeks' gestation. The doctor ran blood tests and other tests. Then, after an ultrasound, he seemed to confirm our worst fears. He told us through a translator, to prepare Chris and me for having a blighted ovum or a molar pregnancy because my HCG levels were rising, but that there was no hope this baby would be okay. He stated that the gestational sac was deformed and could *never* support life. Thankfully our translators had not shared the whole story with us until after the fact. They simply said I should be on light bed rest, meaning I could go to class and teach, but could not lift anything or complete work duties. If the bleeding continued, I would be put on complete bed rest. I didn't care what kind of treatment plan I was given. I was going to fight for this little one more than I have ever fought before.

In that time, I was able to delve even deeper into some of my favorite stories of Jesus' healing. The bleeding woman grasping for the hem of His robe, the centurion desperately seeking healing for his servant, the leper kneeling at Jesus' feet asking if He were willing, the widow whose son was brought back to life, all pierced my heart deeper than ever before. In the midst of all of this, my emotions overcame me. I yelled, and screamed, and wept, and begged.

> *"God, you have given and taken away twice now. We weren't even trying for this baby. Please don't take this one too. You know how heavy my heart is. Yes, you are still good, but please let me touch the hem of your robe. If you are willing, you can make us well. Just say the word and it will be done. You alone hold the power to raise what was pronounced dead back to life. You are our hope, and if you give us this baby to hold in our arms, I will forever tell of your Holy power."*

Chris and I decided it was time to tell the rest of those with whom we were living on the base to also pray for our miracle. We refused to give up the fight but knew we couldn't fight alone. We needed other fellow believers to keep our arms lifted like Aaron and Hurr did for Moses in the midst of the weariness of battle (Exodus 17:11-13). A vast number of people from around the nations prayed. Even a twelve-year-old decided he would fast until we knew that this baby was okay. Everyone stood with us, holding our arms up as we continued to fight for life. So, when I started bleeding again the following week, there was a tangible silence, as it felt like *everyone* held their breath. I returned to that hospital again. I had hope in my heart and desperately refused to let the fear creep in.

Chris was unable to accompany me at this time as it was his turn to teach the lesson, and no others had been prepared to cover him. For whatever reason, we were both at peace with him remaining on the base while some of our beautiful Khmer family took me once again to face the doctor. After relaying that I was bleeding yet again, he started the scan. To his visible surprise, the sac was perfectly formed once again, and that tiny little peanut was perfect, measuring exactly as she should have been. In Khmer, he gasped in disbelief, "Oh! There's a baby in there!" He also called this babe a miracle baby and told me to invite him to her birthday party so he could bring this miracle baby some gifts. I sobbed tears of relief, joy, and gratitude the entire way back to the base. In fact, all of our students saw me crying and thought the worst until I showed Chris the ultrasound, and he in turn showed them. Again, the atmosphere was tangible, but this time with utter joy as word spread, and we told everyone of God's power! I finally had my miracle. God finally said, "Yes!" And I finally saw my tiny little perfect peanut!

The weeks to follow presented themselves with multiple other battles against fear; each time I had to remind myself, and had to be reminded by others, that God had *already* performed the miracle of giving life. I had to trust it was for a reason, and I would indeed see and hold my baby on this side of eternity.

At ten weeks' gestation, I saw our little peanut with her arms and legs flailing, and finally heard the heartbeat we had so longed to hear. A sweet Khmer friend, Sopheap, joined me and filmed the ultrasound so that we could show Chris, who, once again, had to teach in the school. Then, at eleven weeks, the bleeding began again out of nowhere. However, again, we returned from the hospital visit with another incredible little ultrasound picture depicting the beautiful life quickly, yet perfectly forming within me.

With this rainbow pregnancy, I experienced many more minor complications-an abscess, a UTI, hemorrhoids, the works. With each passing symptom, again, I was incredibly grateful for the signs that my little baby girl was still developing as she should have been. I continuously stated with a smile on my face, "I prayed for this."

Chris and I returned back to the Philippines after our three-month school in Cambodia had finished, but this time, we stayed in a base in Cebu. It was surreal being in my second trimester in the same country within which just months before I had experienced such grief and heartache. I was immediately set up with an OB just a brief Jeepney ride away. This OB completely understood the battle with anxiety I was facing. She sympathized with me and was always elated to find that baby's strong heartbeat. By this time, in the States, we would have known the gender by now, and consequently been able to name the baby. We were already praying for this baby daily, and talking to them, telling many of Jesus' stories, etc. However, this was a part of pregnancy I had never been able to experience with Sammy and Micah. I felt the tiny little flutters, turned to kicks, turned to arms and legs flailing everywhere, and I loved every second of it. My belly was growing by the minute, and I was overjoyed to go to the mall to purchase maternity clothing I had been longing to need for so long. By twenty weeks, Chris and my wedding anniversary was coming, and we really hoped to have a gender reveal on that day. We spent the week prior calling and traveling all over Cebu to find someone who could make our dreams come true. After trying about four different places, we got a hold of someone who could see me the same day if I had a prescription from my doctor to have an anatomy scan completed. Now, with closing time less than thirty minutes away, and my OB not answering her phone because she was with patients all day, it was a race against time. However, with prayer, and some speedy taxi drivers, Juvy, one of my closest friends in ministry who had been with us in Las Montañas, Baguio, Cambodia, and now Cebu, gripped the sealed envelope with the baby's gender in her hands. We happily handed over some brightly colored Philippine pesos to her to set up the reveal, and at last experienced the intense joy and anticipation of wondering what color we would see.

Just a few days later, on November 12th, our anniversary, Juvy and some of the other incredible base staff set up the most beautiful gender reveal party. They honored us for our anniversary with flowers, and a huge basket of fruit, then popped the confetti cannons revealing that our little Hosanna was indeed coming! The entire base had celebrated, choosing their colors to wear between blue and pink. Of course, we would have been thrilled to see blue confetti as the Lord had already given us our desire: a healthy baby. Our time in Cebu, despite the various health challenges, was one of joyous celebration. This seemed the direct antithesis to my first trimester filled with fighting anxiety and fear. Things were finally looking up!

Then, upon returning to the States that December just before the third trimester had begun, I scheduled my first appointment with the same OB who had treated me after Sammy had passed. "Congratulations!" She greeted me with a warm embrace, and tears in her eyes. "I told you there was hope!" However, after another anatomy scan, and briefly detailing my family history, she classified my pregnancy as high-risk due to the previous losses, and the fact that Chris was born with both a blood disorder as well as a heart condition. This meant I was to be closely monitored with a series of level two ultrasounds in another town, an hour drive away every couple of weeks until Hosanna was to be born. I knew she was safe, so my thoughts were, *more opportunities to see my growing baby!*

In the months leading up to her birth, we had scares of her not moving for over a couple hours, my water possibly breaking early (thankfully I had just peed myself), and a misdiagnosis of a UTI, which was later discovered while I was in labor to be two 7mm kidney stones. Through it all, the Lord was and always is faithful. He had already performed the miracle of bringing what was pronounced dead back to life. He even redeemed my experience with Pregnancy Care as I not only became a client but was invited to share Hosanna's story at their annual banquet as the honored guest speaker just weeks before she was due. Additionally, He had spoken my love language, yet again, through many gifts, but especially a pea pod necklace that remains very dear to my heart to this day. A sweet friend, Dee, had gifted it to me when she found out I was pregnant with my rainbow. It has two white pearls, and then a rainbow bead within a wire pea pod representing my babies. It served then as a daily reminder of the miracle He had performed, and the hope that this baby would be healthy, in my arms shortly.

The Tuesday before giving birth, I was exactly at thirty-nine weeks' gestation and Chris and I sped to Labor and Delivery because I was peeing blood. I was terrified, but little Hosanna was quick to move around and let me know she was still healthy. The OB on call briefly glanced at the sample I left and diagnosed me with having a UTI. *That was fast. Did he even test it?* He sent me home with antibiotics before I even had time to vocalize these thoughts, but not before the hospital staff curtly warned me that Covid restrictions were tightening, and I would only be able to have my husband with me in labor and delivery. No. One. Else.

I was shocked, to say the least. For the two weeks prior, I had called my doctor every other day to ensure that my mom and my husband would be allowed with me to help me through everything. They were key components of my birth plan. For two weeks, I was reassured that each labor and delivery patient was allowed to be accompanied with two support people. I already had to let go of the fantasy that my dad would be there at my head, taking pictures of the first look, and that members of Chris' and my family would be able to visit in the hospital. *Now this?! I can't have my mommy?!* The morning of the day I went into the hospital for the supposed UTI, the rules changed, and there was threat that they would likely change again to just me allowed in Labor and Delivery. In the midst of all this hysteria, Labor and Delivery was very short on supplies, too. I had once heard that you can take pretty much anything to help, but now, it was hard enough to even find toilet paper and hand sanitizer! My idea of my birth of the miracle baby seemed to break by the minute.

Then, very early Thursday morning, I awoke screaming in excruciating pain. Chris, thinking I had yet another Charley horse (those occurred nightly during the third trimester) prepared to give me a leg massage, but I couldn't move at all. I remember thinking and yelling, "This is NOT labor!" In order to get out of bed, Chris had to support me sitting up, and then I physically had to lift up my right leg with both my hands. I gimped into the emergency waiting room wincing at every minuscule movement, and the reaction was the same. "Oh, you must be in labor!" But I knew better. This pain did *not* come in waves. It was not what had always been described, and it was not what I had experienced with Sammy. *This* pain was unyielding.

In the Labor and Delivery triage, I began peeing blood once again, but was barely contracting. The nurses were completely baffled. All the while, through tears and huffs of trying to catch a breath, I pleaded for pain medication. I was not in labor. There was no music or muscle pressure or stretch to help me to work with contractions as I had been taught. My OB was the one on-call in the hospital that night, and she sent me to have an ultrasound to both make sure Hosanna was still doing well, and to diagnose the cause of the pain. After what felt like an eternity of waiting and writhing, she appeared and told me she had good news and bad news. The good news was that I was not leaving without my baby. She was going to induce me first thing in the morning after the antibiotics cleared out of my system, and I had time to rest on pregnancy-safe pain medication for the stones. But the bad news was that I would also be having surgery to break up the rather large kidney stones that were causing me to be in that much distress. To top everything off, not only was my husband the only one allowed with me in the hospital as Covid rules had gone even further into effect while I was writhing in pain, but he was not allowed to *leave* the hospital for anything. If he did, he would risk not being allowed to return. At that point, I didn't care. My baby was going to fill my empty arms at last!

Friday night, March 20th, 2020, after about twelve hours of labor, the nurse checked me and told me it was time to do some practice pushes. After about two practice pushes, the words I had been eagerly waiting to hear finally rang throughout the entire room. "Okay, stop pushing. It's time to page your doctor. Hosanna is coming!" Immediately, I couldn't contain my elation, so I began to sob. Blinking through teary eyes, I spied Chris on the phone with my mom, telling her to drop what she was doing and bring my dad. Then he teared up as well. Five and a half pushes later, Hosanna Hope (meaning "Praise the Lord of Hope") was finally born. My parents witnessed the first cries while they set up bar stools in the rain right outside my window with a welcome sign pressed up against it. It was still too hard to see, so after she was born and cleaned up, Chris Facetimed them to keep some sense of whatever normalcy we could grasp. The weight of physically holding the 8-pound, 2-ounce little miracle God gave me, brought emotion from the very depths of my soul as I wept tears of joy and gratitude.

***

Chris:

Being in Cambodia felt like a fresh start as we were there with friends that we had met in Las Montañas. Two of our friends are a married Khmer couple, Ngim and Dara, with whom we had stayed for the first few weeks. Bong Dara, the husband is an amazing friend and leader, and he knew the struggles that we had been going through. The first day there, he leaned into me and said, "I am so happy you guys are staying here. Everyone that has trouble getting pregnant stays here and gets pregnant with a healthy baby, bro!" I couldn't help but laugh at his suggestion and encouragement. God had been restoring the Khmer lands and little did I know that it was here that He would restore our hearts, among people who truly loved the Lord. Cambodia is a land of 'hope'.

In no time, Denelle became pregnant with our little baby, made in Cambodia with American parts. During the first complication, I had to stay in the hallway of the doctor's office and couldn't even go in, once again. For some reason, I did not feel anxious or panicked. I wouldn't say my faith was so great, but rather I had become partially numb. I believe it was that same night that the whole base had a community worship night. Either way, whenever the event was, hundreds of Khmer people surrounded Denelle in prayer and stood firm in their belief that we would have a healthy baby. After that night, I had some sense of the truth God was going to speak over us.

I never got to see my peanut while in Cambodia, only the ultrasound that Denelle showed me after her confirmation. I had stayed behind to teach that day, and Denelle went to get checked again after some bleeding. Class had ended, and I waited for her to message me back on my spotty wifi signal. Surrounded by Bong Dara with whom we stayed, and another new friend from the class we were running, Bong Samphas, I finally received Denelle's message as it came through. All it said was, "There's a baby!" I instantly cried, and my two friends behind me feared that I had heard the worst. I turned around and declared "There's a baby!" My friends' eyes flooded with tears of joy, and they jumped up and down in celebration with me. At the moment I received the message, Denelle victoriously came through the gates of the base as we all ran down to greet her. We celebrated together as I held the ultrasound! It was finally happening; it was time for Baby Scanlan to grow and come to fulfill God's promise.

I don't ever remember being upset about having to accommodate my wife's new food aversions, or hormone swings, being pregnant, even if it meant eating my potato chips outside in the rain so she wouldn't hear my chewing, even though *she* was eating chips as well. Every morning, I would go down to see what was for breakfast or lunch, let Denelle know, and then see if she would need something else. One evening, just before dark, I was given the task of scouring Cambodia for macaroni and cheese and milk to satisfy my wife's insatiable cravings. Over the next few weeks in Cambodia, we would come to a greater understanding of God and his promises. Hosanna was coming!

After some time, we went back to the Philippines after the Khmer school was over, and we were asked to help staff another in Cebu. While there, I finally got my first glance at our miracle baby. At the ultrasound, I was like a kid who got the perfect Christmas gift that he wasn't expecting. I honestly don't know what I was expecting, but I definitely wasn't prepared to see her little peanut shape and little arms and legs flailing at the sack she was in. It was absolutely perfect. "Ah! The baby's kicking you! Did you see that? Did you feel that?" I was giddy with joy.

At this point, we still didn't know the gender of our baby but we both had a strong feeling. Every night Denelle and I would talk to our little miracle and wait to feel those little kicks and to see the occasional foot sticking out. On mine and Denelle's wedding anniversary, the whole base in Cebu set up a rather large gender reveal party while we finished with class. We came to find a decorated canopy for us to sit under, a huge fruit basket, a great lunch, and our school leader, who was eagerly waiting to help us find out the gender. Almost all of the base community was dressed in either pink or blue, and celebrated with us as we learned our baby was a little girl! A week or so later, we would settle on our baby girl's name; Hosanna Hope Scanlan. Hosanna was coming!

Your turn: Has God given you your rainbow? If not, how has He restored your hope?

14

The World Made Right

Early in my pregnancy with Hosanna, in the midst of the uncertainties and complications, I had a dream. When waking up from the dream, I did not remember most of the details, but what I *can* say is that I was in labor with my baby girl, and nothing was going right. The world outside us was falling apart, my birth plan went out the window, it seemed like everything was in tangible chaos. However, in the dream, the very second my baby girl was placed into my arms, the world around me stilled, and the atmosphere of chaos melted away to make room for peace.

When Hosanna was born at the very beginning of the pandemic, the entire world seemed to shut down. We were supposed to continue forward in world missions with Word by Heart, but instead we were jobless and found ourselves living with my parents indefinitely. We lost most of the mission support we had gained, and understandably so. Furthermore, no one was hiring at the time because unless considered an essential worker, everyone was ordered to stay at home. The air reeked of anxiety and uncertainty. The anxiety caused me to fear random things, like the times I would wake in the night frantically searching for my baby. Out of dead sleep, or as dead sleep as one can be in with a newborn, I sat up, thumped the middle of the bed, and yelled, "Where's my baby?!" This happened multiple times a night for many nights to follow, even though she was *always* in the crib where she had been placed less than two hours prior.

Additionally, due to complications, severe reflux, and other unknown factors, Hosanna would not nurse, and constantly teetered the "failure to thrive" line, even with bottle-feeding. To top it all off, I was diagnosed with Hashimoto's disease, and Hosanna was diagnosed with a bilateral aortic valve, making everyone in my parents' household high-risk for contracting Covid and experiencing severe symptoms.

Everything I had ever envisioned when welcoming my baby into the world with other friends and family members visiting, turned swiftly into visits with a window between us. Only immediate family members were allowed to visit inside, provided they wore a mask. The postpartum anxiety mixed with the hysteria of this new virus caused such uncertainty that I required my mother-in-law to quarantine for two weeks, not even stepping off her land in order to come visit our little miracle for an overnight stay without a mask. I suffered immensely from anxiety to the point that I required anyone, including myself, who had come from the *outside* world to change clothes and shower immediately after returning home *before* coming within feet of this tiny baby. My dad and husband had set up a disinfection station in our garage for each time they brought something from the store inside.

And when Hosanna was a few months old, I was asked to accompany my mom to my all-time favorite store to try to fend off the anxiety. The plan backfired, and resulted in me freaking out in one of the aisles as I simply froze in place and cried, even though Hosanna was safe and sound with her daddy at home.

Despite *everything* around me, each time I held my little miracle, all was made right in the world. All the chaos and anxiety melted away into the background, and nothing else mattered at that point. My arms and heart were finally full.

***

Chris:

"Hosanna is coming," soon turned into, "Hosanna is here!" Time flew as we shared Word By Heart stories and waited for our miracle. We stayed in the hospital for three days while Denelle dealt with her kidney stones and prepared to give birth and fill her arms with what she had been longing for. The world shut down around us while we were there, but it never stopped our joy that was coming.

After Denelle rested, on the second day, the nurse came in to check on her and told us that Denelle was ready to have her baby girl, and the doctor was on the way. If we wanted anyone to come and sit outside the window to hear their grand baby being born, now was the time to call. Denelle's parents had barely arrived, and were on speaker phone, when Hosanna was born. Her mom desperately desired to hear that first cry. After the world settled a little bit, we video called them to see their granddaughter! We were thrilled our miracle had arrived, but sad at the same time, as we couldn't have anyone come visit us and meet her. I remember the first night Hosanna was born, the nurse handed her to me while Denelle slept. My precious daughter simply looked up at me, and I repeated the phrase I had said to her dozens of times while she was in Denelle's womb. My baby just continued to look at me and fell asleep in my arms as I prayed for her. My heart was full.

Then, reality hit again, when I left the hospital to retrieve my baby's car seat to bring my family home. The security guard stopped me because the date on my bracelet was not that date. It was from three days prior. Despite my valiant, yet sleep-deprived efforts to explain that I was trying to take everyone home, it took a Labor and Delivery nurse coming off-shift to convince the guard to let me pass with the words, "Uh, he's getting his *baby*!"

Over the next few weeks, Covid was in full rage, and many of our friends and family members had to visit Hosanna through the front window of Denelle's parents' house. Even with the madness of the pandemic bombarding us everyday, we found joy in watching our little one grow into the smart, beautiful, and prayerful little miss that she is now.

15

The Widow of Nain

One of my favorite stories we learned while in the school in Las Montañas is the Widow of Nain found in Luke 7:11-17.

"Soon afterward Jesus went with his disciples to the village of Nain, and a large crowd followed him. A funeral procession was coming out as he approached the village gate. The young man who had died was a widow's only son, and a large crowd from the village was with her. When the Lord saw her, His heart overflowed with compassion. "Don't cry." He said. Then he walked over to the coffin and touched it, and the bearers stopped. "Young man," He said, "I tell you, get up." Then the dead boy sat up and began to talk! And Jesus gave him back to his mother. Great fear swept the crowd, and they praised God, saying, "A mighty prophet has risen among us," and

"God has visited his people today." And the news about Jesus spread throughout Judea and the surrounding countryside."

(Luke 17:11-17 NLT)

It's short, and maybe takes a minute or so to read, so if you read the Bible quickly, or at a surface-level, it's really easy to skip over the incredible impact this story holds. But throughout the battle on my knees for Micah, and then for Hosanna, this story became more real to me than ever before. I felt like the widow, simply hopeless and broken. Then Jesus saw me and spoke hope into my heart when He told me, "Don't cry." Then, He touched my womb, speaking life into it, and telling Hosanna to "Get up." It was then that the doctor saw that the womb had a perfectly formed little peanut within the healed amniotic sac. When Hosanna Hope was placed into my arms, that's the part in the story when Jesus gave the boy back to his mother.

Now, when I share this little Bible story, I feel immense hope, and I share it as my own testimony. Don't get me wrong, the Bible isn't about me. It's about Jesus, but He made that widow's story incredibly personal to me through how He acted within my own story.

***

Chris

"At the sound of Mary's greeting, Elizabeth's child leaped within her, and Elizabeth was filled with the Holy Spirit. Elizabeth gave a glad cry and exclaimed to Mary, "God has blessed you above all women, and your child is blessed. Why am I so honored that the mother of my Lord should visit me? When I heard your greeting, the baby in my womb jumped for joy. You are blessed because you believed that the Lord would do what he said.""

(Luke 1:41-45 NLT)

While in Cambodia, Denelle and I spent time learning new stories with the Word by Heart method. While she focused on Jesus' stories of healing, I started learning all the stories surrounding Jesus' birth before

His baptism. Our baby growing inside her mommy was definitely not the prophesied Messiah *at all*, but there's something about telling the story to a room full of people and locking eyes with your wife when you speak the last line. It rings true for her as well. You see her faithfulness, then all the pain she had endured slips away, even for just a moment. In no way do I want to twist scripture, but in those moments that passage could have been written:

> "Jesus gave a glad cry and exclaimed to Denelle, 'I have blessed you and your child is blessed.'
>
> Us: 'Why should we be so honored that our Lord would bless us with a healthy baby? When we heard her heartbeat, the baby in her womb kicked for joy.'
>
> Jesus: 'You are blessed because you believed that I would do what I said.'

Again, I definitely don't want to twist scripture, or make it about myself, but the Lord has a way of using the Living Word to speak to our hearts and bring more depth to His story within us. It's been four years since learning the story and seeing God's hope restore our souls with the hope of having children. Yet, I still get emotional telling the Bible story, especially seeing the fullness of His faithfulness in front of my eyes.

Your Turn: Reflect on either of these small stories, or one you have read. How does God speak hope to you through them? What do you learn of His faithfulness?

16

A Little Pot of Gold

Just before Hosanna turned two years old, Chris and I had decided to stop preventing possible pregnancy again. It took a lot to get to that point again as we both had to find full-time jobs so we could afford to start over and move out on our own. We had to accumulate vehicles to get to and from work and other necessary places, and we had to save up to afford an in-home babysitter/nanny. But we were finally in a place where it seemed possible. We didn't tell anyone, including Hosanna, that we were going to let things happen if God intended them to.

At this point, our tiny tot had developed a slight obsession with all things baby. She owned over twenty different baby dolls (most of them were given to her once people had discovered her love for them), and she took good care of every single one. She also seemed to have a more mature grasp of what it meant when a mama had a baby "in her tummy." She had been to a couple baby showers and had seen many of her parents' friends go from having a baby in their tummies to having a baby to hold. But nothing prepared us for what she revealed one night after her aunt's baby shower.

The three of us were laying in bed reading our Bible stories as our usual nightly routine, but this time, she kept saying, "Baby." We thought she was asking for one of her many baby dolls, so we handed her her favorite, then tried to continue reading. "No; baby," she refuted. So, we tried another, and another. Finally, we asked her where the baby was that she wanted. Hosanna lifted my shirt, rubbed my belly, gave it a kiss, and stated, "In Mommy's tummy." Flabbergasted, we repeated the question, "Where's the baby?" Then we followed by asking, "Can you kiss the baby?" And again, she kissed my stomach. I honestly can't recall what happened next as we were dumbfounded to say the least, however, in my mind, I knew it was too early to test.

The next day began like any other Sunday. Chris had brought me my favorite Starbucks drink, and we were relaxing at home. We weren't going to church that day because Chris' mom was in town and was going to visit during that time. I thought only a little more of what Hosanna had said, but then highly considered it once I took a drink of my Açaí. Almost instantly, I had heartburn. Before that time, the only time I ever had heartburn was when I was pregnant. *Could she actually know I'm pregnant? If I'm having symptoms, it might not be too early to test.*

Without Chris' knowledge, I drove to the dollar store to pick up some tests; all the while convincing myself I was insane to take the word of my *toddler*. When I returned home, I took the test immediately. Any woman who has looked up ways to conceive knows that when taking a pregnancy test, the most accurate time to take it is during the first morning urination. By this time, it was almost lunchtime. I was a couple days away from Aunt Flow's scheduled visit, and I took it in the middle of the day, yet those two pink lines revealed themselves almost immediately! I was so surprised, I accidentally knocked over the cup of urine into the sink. I gripped that little test, gasping that my daughter was *right*! Then, I came back to reality, when I decided to try a second test and realized my sample had spilled down the drain.

I hadn't been able to surprise Chris with the other three pregnancies, but I wanted to this time. However, I needed help, so I messaged someone I knew he wouldn't be upset if she knew before him. Almost immediately, Lynzee, a fellow rainbow mom friend of mine, helped me devise a plan to have her make a shirt for Hosanna to announce she was a big sister. I made some excuse to go to her house for a few minutes, gulping down bottles of water so I could take a second test just to be sure, and Lynzee made the shirt while I took a second test. The second test, which was a very diluted sample, revealed I wasn't losing it. After showing Lynzee, she presented me with the shirt, then recommended I wait until I could take another test in a couple days. The shirt read, "I was right. I'm a big sister!" If you know me, I'm *not* patient when it comes to surprises, so I *had* to tell him right away. I stole Hosanna away into her room, while Chris and his mother looked confused at the suddenness of everything. I think I said something like, "Lynzee was just really excited to give Hosanna a shirt and couldn't wait. She asked me to take a picture of her in it right away." As she toddled out into the living room, Chris read the words, increasing in volume at each syllable he read aloud. The look of surprise and joy on his face when he read her shirt was one, I will never forget. I was shocked, excited, nervous, and fighting anxious thoughts like never before, and I *still* had to deal with the heartburn from earlier.

The next day, I scheduled an appointment with my OB because when I had been diagnosed with Hashimoto's disease, I was directed by my ENT and OB to have a blood test immediately if I were to become pregnant again. I knew I was extremely early in this pregnancy, so I asked for my doctor to withhold any internal ultrasounds and exams until I would be able to hear my baby's heartbeat. I knew that if something caused irritation, and I couldn't have that reassuring beat, I would be a wreck. Thankfully, my OB has an incredibly compassionate heart and agreed to wait at least two weeks. In the meantime, she ran blood tests and checked my vitals.

The day of my first ultrasound two long weeks later, I was shaking in every part of my body. It seemed like a familiar scene. Chris unfortunately had to work, so my mom and my dad picked me up in their blue pickup truck. Hosanna was with her nanny, antsy for her mommy to come home and tell her about the baby. My mom and dad waited anxiously in the car while I walked alone (Covid restrictions had become tighter again at the time), my feet were feeling heavier and heavier with each step. Again, my heart could be seen bursting through my chest as Sue, the ultrasound technician, prepared the wand.

To my relief, I heard the heartbeat first, almost immediately, strong and unmistakable. Then, I recognized that beautiful little blob that most cannot make out. I knew it was my pot of gold. Immense peace flooded every cell of my being! Then, I heard Sue tell me she needed to get the scans to my doctor. But there was a hint of reservation in her soft voice. She left me not knowing anything about this little baby. Normally, she would celebrate with me, ask me what pictures I wanted printed, give me my envelope of pictures, then send me on my way to my OB waiting room. She returned after another incredibly long wait to tell me that my baby was doing great, but there was a rather large bleed behind the placenta that was threatening the pregnancy as a whole. "What does this mean? Is my baby going to be okay? I nervously questioned, dreading having to relay this news multiple times as I was trying to process. All she could tell me was that its presence threatened the pregnancy as a whole, and the doctor was upping my progesterone prescription. This time it felt as though the anxious thoughts were physically pummeling down on top of me, and I was losing the strength to fight them.

After setting up another ultrasound appointment for the following week and being placed essentially on bed rest with many restrictions to what I could do, I drug my feet to my parents in the parking lot, my mind racing. To my surprise, I also met Chris, who had been allowed to take a few minutes off work to hear the news himself. After relaying everything Sue had shared, and showing the video and photos to everyone, we all immediately prayed, then turned our thoughts toward that strong heartbeat. Again, Jesus had already performed the miracle of healing my womb. We had to remain immovable in faith. My mom always used the heartbeat theory to predict whether the baby is a girl or boy, so to keep hope, she started talking about me having a little boy. The heartbeat was on the slower end of the healthy spectrum. It was much better to think about that than the news I had been given.

I was scheduled for a total of three weeks of ultrasounds back-to-back until everything finally appeared hopeful. The bleed had slowly been diminishing in size each week, and thankfully I never actually bled out. But those three weeks were painful while I was constantly wondering once again what was going to happen to my little one. My heart was not fully distraught, though, as God was giving me His peace. I knew something serious was happening, but I knew that this little baby was going to be okay. In one of the ultrasounds, my tiny peanut appeared to be dancing on his head and reassuring me he was going to stay strong and keep fighting. Nightly, our little family of three prayed over that little dancing blob in my womb, with Hosanna always taking the beginning of the prayer, asking that the baby was "healfy and safe and gwowing".

Finally at eleven weeks' gestation, I saw my OB, received all clear, and was given my pregnancy packet. Prior to that, she couldn't confirm that this pregnancy was viable with the bleed as large and in the position it was. *Thank God she never said that before now.* However, the pregnancy complications for my pot of gold were far from over. Just after that visit, Chris, Hosanna and I had all been diagnosed with round two of Covid. This was the easiest round for Hosanna and Chris, but it was another story for me. Of course, Hezekiah was much too small to feel his movements to be reassured that he was not affected. However, I could *swear* that I felt those familiar little bubbles in one side of my tummy. *I wonder if it's God's way of calming my heart once again, telling me that this baby is okay.*

One particular day during round two, I became so faint that I had to sit on the floor in the shower in order not to lose consciousness. I immediately called my OB and measured my blood oxygen level. She told me that anything ninety-five or lower warranted an immediate visit to the ER. I was at a ninety-six at that point. Despite how I was feeling, I *had* to know that my pot of gold was okay, and I had to do all in my ability to take care of us. That day, I pulled out the at-home Doppler I had purchased when pregnant with Hosanna, and to my relief, I located my baby's heartbeat immediately! Then, I scheduled an at-home IV treatment to hopefully gain strength. The next few days were miserable, but I knew that my baby was okay as I could always find his heartbeat and discern from my own. Then, as soon as I was able, I scheduled a visit to confirm what I already knew in my heart. This baby was a strong fighter because his strength came from the Lord.

About two-thirds of the way through pregnancy, I was sent to Phoenix, a four-hour drive from Lake Havasu to complete my anatomy scan as my previous high-risk OB had closed his practice indefinitely due to an injury. Remember the heart condition and blood condition for which they looked at Hosanna? It was now my little boy's time. The technician took well over an hour to scan everything, especially the heart, to make sure nothing was amiss. It appeared to be such a positive scan that I was completely in shock when the doctor relayed to me that the placenta was looking larger than it should, and that my little baby boy was measuring on the smaller end. The doctor explaining the results told me that there was a very real possibility of needing to be induced earlier than thirty-seven weeks if the placenta was indeed affecting his growth. *Here we go again*! Anxiety began to loom once more, as I became high-risk once again. However, despite everything, Hosanna never skipped a beat when praying for her brother to be "healfy and safe and gwowing."

Back home, Sue the technician saw me once again to check on the health of my boy shortly after that anatomy scan. Thankfully, this time, which was now about a month prior to my due date, I was issued a clean bill of health for both me and for that little pot of gold. Well, clean except that he had turned to a breech position. I honestly had gotten used to good news speckled with not-so-great news that I was not shocked in the least. I prepared my heart to have a c-section if he did not turn. I asked Jesus to give peace to my heart, and asked friends who have endured c-sections about what I might expect. I never gave up hope that he could still turn, but at the same time, I wanted to be ready and at peace if it came to that scenario. My only birth plan was "Healthy baby, and healthy mama." Thankfully, after prayer and some stretching, little Hezekiah flipped once again, and I found myself in the doctor's office for once with only good news at thirty-eight weeks. The placenta was still larger than normal, but Hezekiah's growth was on par for what he should be, his heartbeat remained strong, and movements consistent. My OB joked, "Congratulations! You're boring. I'm no longer worried!" She knew I had gotten used to her being concerned about many different aspects, so she figured it would lift my spirits going into the final countdown until he was to be born.

I have pondered many times about what happened next, but I have never arrived at an answer why. After being told my son was head down, still measuring a little small, but a healthy size, and that I was slightly dilated and 75% effaced, I began to weep and tremble. It was almost as if I had become so accustomed to the good-news-bad-news talk that once it was *all* good, I could not accept that was the case. It felt as though I was waiting for the bad news the doctor was keeping from me. *"But..."* The anxiety I had fought so hard all pregnancy to fend off had completely overtaken me. I experienced the overwhelming need to hold my son in my hands on the outside to know that he truly was okay. In an attempt to put my heart at ease, my OB set me up on a stress test to monitor the heartbeat as well as any contractions I was experiencing. Hezekiah was strong and healthy, moving around to reassure me he was okay. He even kicked the monitor so much that the nurse had a very hard time trying to keep it on my stomach. I tried to envision holding this precious miracle in my hands very soon. Then, my OB reassured me that if the anxiety becomes too strong to bear, she would be willing to induce me once it's safe at thirty-nine weeks. She understood that with my history, I needed that option. As I weighed all options, in my heart, I decided that induction was slightly better than having to live with the overbearing weight of anxiety on my shoulders.

That day, Friday, I broke down more times than I can count, crushed from the anxious need to physically see my baby was okay. Thankfully, I wouldn't have to wait long. In an odd turn of events, my cousin's memorial was that weekend, bringing my parents home from the Northeast one week earlier than they had planned, and my brother home for the weekend. The memorial was Saturday night, and then we decided to dress up in our costumes to partake in the Fall Fun Fair. Hosanna had chosen our costume theme to be Monsters Inc. So, I wheeled little Boo from Monsters Inc around in our foldable red wagon as a heavily pregnant Mike, holding hands with a very furry Sulley. As a family, with my parents and brother in tow, we took pictures, had lots of laughs, and let the grief from earlier melt off of us. No sooner than Chris, Hosanna and I had arrived home, and they had changed out of their costumes, my belly started hardening like that of shell chocolate poured onto ice cream. Then the pain increased, so I forgot to change out of my costume. Chris put Hosanna to bed because I was too big and too uncomfortable to waddle to her tiny bed, then get up off the floor. As he lay with her, trying to get her to sleep, I started timing my contractions, and knew it was time! Still dressed as Mike, I raced to Hosanna's bedroom, woke my husband, and directed him to call my mom to meet us at the hospital, and my dad to watch Hosanna, who had only just fallen asleep, then we swiped the hospital bags.

I don't think any of the hospital staff thought I would be admitted because of how I acted, still dressed as Mike, but I was four-five centimeters already, and almost fully effaced. When Chris went to fetch the bags, the receptionists commented on their shock that it was time. I was smiling, at peace, and only wincing at the contraction pain though they were indeed very close and very big according to the monitors.

Little Hezekiah Jude (meaning "My strength comes from the Lord, so I praise Him") Scanlan was born Sunday afternoon, just hours before my parents were set to take my brother back to the airport for his trip back home. My mom had been in the hospital with my husband and me since Saturday night, when I went into labor, and my dad had brought my brother to see me off. They both arrived at my room just as the nurse darted out to get the doctor because it was time. My pot of gold was born in no time at all, just four and one half pushes later on October 30th, 2022, in the same room our rainbow was born. But this time, my family (minus Hosanna) was all present in the room to greet him. As the doctor stitched me up, she found the clots behind the placenta that had once threatened my strong baby boy. She cleaned them out, remarking, "Thank God you got the epidural. This would be more painful than childbirth if not." Then she made sure I was healthy as my parents and husband passed around my tiny boy. I reflected on all that had happened and laughed as I realized that Saturday morning that I had gone into labor, Hosanna counted to fourteen, skipping number thirteen and said, "Kai Kai come out." I was in labor for about fourteen hours, with the thirteenth hour a crazy whirlwind, and then Kai Kai came out. I continued to reflect with complete gratitude that my boy was finally here and healthy, as Hezekiah was passed around to meet his family.

However, when he was returned back to my arms after meeting everyone, Hezekiah was swiftly turning purple. His faint little newborn coos rapidly turned to gurgles, and Chris raced out of the room without time to even think of using the call button. My little boy was *not* okay. The nurse appeared after sprinting to the room, yanked him out of my arms, and nervously suctioned out his mouth until we heard the gurgle turn back to healthy breathing. The entire ordeal occurred in just a matter of minutes, but it felt like a lifetime as anxious thoughts of him being airlifted to another hospital plagued my mind. To make matters worse, my cousin born earlier the year before was airlifted for the same thing-swallowing and choking on amniotic fluid. Thankfully, our story played out differently, as nurse April, who likely saved my son's life, delicately returned him back into my arms, profusely apologizing for snatching him so swiftly and forcefully. She kept a much closer eye on us throughout our stay. With all well again, my parents left with my brother to take him to the airport while Chris and I gazed at our sweet little boy.

I wish I could say that was the last of the early-life anxiety-ridden moments, but the night of release day, Chris and I found ourselves back in the hospital trembling, overcome once again with anxiety. I had nursed Hezekiah, then laid him down for his first night in the bassinet while Chris and I tried to sleep before our two-hour feeding alarm would go off. Instead, Hezekiah woke us when he started gagging, then gasping for air. Then, suddenly, he couldn't breathe. We set him upright, he spit up, then cleared his airway rather quickly. I hugged him tightly, praying until he fell asleep in my arms, and we turned his head to the side before we laid him back down. After what felt like mere minutes, we heard the familiar sound and sprang to action once again. This time, it took much longer to get him to breathe clearly. I pounded on his back while Chris woke his mom who had been staying in the other room with Hosanna. I thumped on his back for over ten minutes, yet he still struggled to breathe, so Chris did what he saw nurse April do. He grabbed the bulb, then suctioned anything and everything he could from Hezekiah's tiny little mouth. Finally, we could hear his breathing return to normal; and his color flushed back through his tired little body. Perplexed, and terrified of a repeat, Chris and I made the decision to return to the hospital, hoping that a pediatrician on-call from Labor and Delivery might be able to see him, or even better, we could go up to labor and delivery to be treated since we had been released earlier that day.

Because we had worked so hard at home to get Hezekiah's breathing returned to normal, he was no longer considered "emergent," so we anxiously waited behind a long list of patients for over two hours. Thankfully the medic in triage put our hearts at peace by telling us his oxygen level was healthy, color good, and lungs sounded clear. Then he informed us that we weren't going to be seen by any pediatricians, so since we had a scheduled appointment with ours the very next day, we decided to return home. Chris planned to stay up all night so Hezekiah could sleep peacefully upright. The rest of the night, we had one more incident, but Chris, who had chugged a Red Bull to stay awake, handled it immediately.

The next morning, mere hours after the last incident, delirious from sleep deprivation and anxiety, we recapped the events of the night to his pediatrician, who suggested our pot of gold might be experiencing reflux due to a tongue tie. It must have been serious enough as the nurse was able to get us into an ENT that same day to clip the tie. In fact, by the time we had returned home, about a ten-minute drive away, Chris and I both had missed calls on our phones from the nurse telling us that she had arranged an appointment in a few hours. And since that appointment to get the tie clipped, Hezekiah has not had another incident. Now, he is the most joyful little mama's boy anyone has ever met, and he loves nursing and mealtime almost as much as he loves his big sister. Most importantly, time after time, he has gone through many moments that proved his strength truly does come from the Lord.

***

Chris:

"Oh, my little dude!" I heard myself nearly yell these words as the doctor lifted Hezekiah into the air and onto his mother's chest. He was finally here! The night of Denelle's cousin's memorial, we decided to take Hosanna to the Fall Fun Fair as we weren't planning on taking her trick or treating. Shortly after arriving home, we got Hosanna down for bed. As soon as I got Hosanna to sleep, I drifted off too. Then, Denelle woke me. She looked at me and said she thought it was time. I barely had enough time to wake up and realize what she had said before we headed to the hospital, with all of our baby gear and Denelle's mom. Her dad stayed with Hosanna until my mom arrived in the morning.

After Kai Kai was born, the nurse tried to hand me my little man cub, but I declined, not because I didn't want to hold him, but because Covid had robbed Denelle's parents of the opportunity to hold Hosanna in the hospital, and I knew that was a moment that they would cherish. Knowing I would have several moments to hold my son, I offered to let them hold him first. Denelle's mother held him first, then her father, and then me. Of course, I had held his hand and rubbed his back in the heating incubator while Denelle got cleaned, before any of us held him.

Upon taking my little man home, my mother and Hosanna came to the car to greet the newest member of the family. As we settled into the house for the evening, my little girl kissed her baby brother on the head and looked at him with pure love. Even with the future problems we would come to face, the world felt right.

17

Due Dates & Birthdays

There are many very difficult dates for those who have experienced pregnancy loss, but the due dates and the birthdays into heaven are most commonly the most painful. I honestly don't remember much about Sammy's or Micah's due date when they finally arrived for the first time, except tangible peace.

When Sammy's first heavenly birthday came up, Chris and I wanted to start a yearly tradition to bless someone else while we celebrated. We went to our local cake bakery, ordered a cupcake to share, then read Todd Burpo's book, *Heaven is For Real For Kids.* We finished that time with prayer, and imagining how Sammy was celebrating in Heaven. Then, we set out to find someone with the same birthday so that we could pay for their cake or cupcakes in Sammy's honor. We ended up finding one of my old middle school friend's sons. My friend hadn't ordered any cakes or cupcakes yet as she wasn't able to afford much at that time, so it was perfect for us to be able to purchase some cupcakes for her family to celebrate her son. Thankfully, Sammy's birthday was quite a peaceful day. Of course, we shed a few tears, but continuing to acknowledge our sweet heavenly baby was the only thing that seemed right to do. Now, we all celebrate as a family with our children on both Sammy's Heavenly birthday (February 4th) and on Micah's Heavenly birthday (May 25th). We still go to a bakery to pay-it-forward and purchase cupcakes to share. We pray, thanking God for the promise to meet them one day if we accept Jesus, and then we read *Heaven is For Real For Kids* together.

Some have criticized us for talking so openly to our children about their siblings, but the way Hosanna talks about her brother and sister with Jesus is so genuine and so pure. When someone asks her how many siblings she has, she replies with, "I have one sister, and two brothers." And one day, Hosanna broke out into random prayer at the dinner table asking Jesus for a sister soon so that she could have two sisters and two brothers.

Your turn: How do you prepare for the hard days (due dates and/or birthdays)?

18

Pregnancy After Loss (PAL)

Generally, pregnancy brings with it blissful ignorance. Of course, it is known that miscarriages occur, but if my story is any indication, most first-time mothers and fathers do not believe it will happen to them. I am ashamed to admit that when I was pregnant with Sammy, one of my friends from high school experienced an early miscarriage, and my immediate thought was, "*That's heartbreaking, but I am so grateful my baby and I are so covered in prayers that it won't happen to us.*" This happened just two weeks before that devastating hospital visit in Las Montañas.

When I was pregnant with Micah, I did not have that blissful ignorance. Unfortunately, that pregnancy was a fight against fear and anxiety. Looking after wiping, praying I did not see that heartbreaking shade of scarlet, and researching everything I ate down to a piece of chewing gum to ensure that I did not eat anything dangerous to the pregnancy were just a few of the many things that became commonplace in my life. When I was fighting on my knees for Micah, I also had to fight anxiety equally as hard. I could not let the anxious thoughts consume me.

Then, when Jesus finally gave us the miracle for which we had prayed so fervently, I had to fight even harder. Each little step forward was a milestone. When I saw my baby in the ultrasound, that was further than I had been given with either of my other two babies. But anxiety and fear waited, lurking in the shadows. When I heard her heartbeat, I could finally breathe. However, I was still stalked. When Hosanna was kicking me regularly, and my tummy was growing daily, I gained even more footing to defend my heart from the fear and anxiety that were threatening to steal my peace and hope.

With the strength of the Lord, and the faith of my little daughter, I was able to fend off the fear and anxiety with a little less fight when pregnant with Hezekiah. Even with all the good-news-bad-news appointments, I was able to find that peace and hope that I would indeed hold my healthy son and bring him home to his big sister. However, as the pregnancy neared its end, the anxiety ramped up to fight even harder to bring me down, and that time, it almost succeeded.

Pregnancy after loss is not easy by any means. It is a daily decision to trust that God will keep mama and baby "healthy, safe, and growing." And if He doesn't, He's still good. It entails making the choice to fight off the anxious thoughts with hope for the future. One way Chris and I were able to keep fighting was daily celebrating the milestones of the little blessing growing within me, praying over him, and reading God's stories of hope and healing.

Your Turn: What are the tiggers of anxiety and fear that threaten to overtake you? How do you fight against them and keep hope?

19

I Prayed for This

When I was pregnant with Hosanna and Hezekiah, of course it was not without its fair share of uncomfortable and painful symptoms as most pregnancies are. However, I was always so grateful for a healthy baby, that I honestly loved having any and all symptoms. I loved my stretch marks, the hemorrhoids, the morning sickness, the increased acne, the incessant need to pee every half an hour; everything. I loved ultrasounds, every kick, the pain in my ribs when Hosanna was wrapped up in them; everything. If I ever started feeling any disdain, I would verbally remind myself, "*I prayed for this.*" I was incredibly grateful to simply be carrying life within my body. Many pregnant mamas, including myself with Sammy, take for granted all the symptoms of a healthy pregnancy, and can find them to be a negative thing. But those of us who have experienced the pain of having a child in Heaven instead of Earth, know that not everyone who wants this gets this.

After I had lost Sammy, I felt an immense amount of guilt for my attitude. While in our visa-run country when I was still pregnant, Chris and I went clothes shopping because I had very few clothes to wear to keep me warm. I had never liked clothes shopping because I got sticker shock looking at how much money I would be spending for something that I would wear one to two times a week. This time was no different. I wasn't finding anything on which I wanted to spend money, especially supporter money at that, and I didn't think I looked decent in anything I was trying on. At some point, I had become so overstimulated, that I just slammed down the clothes in my hand, and started griping, "It doesn't matter anyway. I'm going to be too fat soon!"

After Sammy was born into Heaven, that attitude was something I deeply regretted. After repenting, I promised myself and God that if I ever was given the opportunity to carry life again, I would be truly joyful in every way I can, and I meant it.

Once I was given the opportunity again with Micah, I wanted to celebrate. I wanted to cherish every minute. For this reason, Chris and I told our closest family and friends immediately after seeing those two pink lines appear. We didn't want to wait. This baby was to be celebrated too. I had hoped that God would give us another baby while we were away, so prior to embarking on our new journey to the Philippines, I had purchased a little blue baby blanket, and I hid it in an Easter egg under the bed in my parents' guest room. As we video chatted with my parents, I had them go on an Easter egg hunt, find the egg under the bed, and then we shared the news. Immediately after that, we celebrated with our Word by Heart students and staff.

In Cambodia, prior to the complications and everything we first experienced with Hosanna, I had disclosed to a friend that I was so excited to be given the opportunity to be pregnant again. Her reaction was surprising as I started dreaming once again about finding out the gender, planning some type of nursery, etc. "Don't get your hopes too high," she warned lovingly. After pondering that statement, I realized there is absolutely no benefit to listening to, "Don't get your hopes up." I had already experienced the most unimaginable pain. Twice. *What is the difference between hoping and allowing myself to dream vs. living in fear and anxiety, guarding my heart from any joy this little life would bring to me?*

When God granted us to be far enough along in pregnancy to hear Hosanna's heartbeat, see her little healthy figure in the ultrasound, and feel her little kicks, it was surreal. Chris and I celebrated with everyone around us because we knew that these precious moments were not guaranteed. When it was time to complete the anatomy scan, and discover our miracle baby's gender, we went through all the hassle simply because we could not wait again for those moments to celebrate.

It was the same with Hezekiah as well. We chose to hope. And we chose to celebrate every little step of the way.

Your turn: Take some time to reflect on attitudes that you might regret having while being blissfully unaware of the grief you'd experience. Is there anything you would take back? How can you grow, and change your mindset? Release that guilt!

20

Sammy's Quilt

When packing up to leavc Las Montañas, I never could have imagined that we would not be returning for a very long time, if ever. I also did not expect to have a baby born into Heaven. I expected to see that little peanut, and then to finish the quilt we had started in Las Montañas as we anxiously waited to return back to staffing the Word by Heart schools. When hurriedly packing to leave, I had gingerly placed the remains of the project with all the other small baby gifts into my suitcase with the hopes to be using them in just a few short months. Arriving at my childhood home, I was still in complete shock, praying that this nightmare would finally end.

After everything had happened, my mom took my suitcases and unpacked for Chris and me. She took the small baby things we had acquired and stored them away somewhere secret for the time we could use them for a baby in our arms. Then she placed the partially made quilt in a cabinet before I was triggered by seeing everything, knowing I'd have to wait even longer for it to be used. Through all the grief, the quilt represented hope lost. It was partially started, but still in many pieces, waiting until the time it could be stitched together. Needless to say, even though I had left with Chris for the Philippines full of hope for a rainbow, the quilt remained behind. It was better to forget that, than to be reminded of everything that it represented. Of course I didn't want to forget my baby, but I didn't want to remember the process of starting the blanket, then continuing to work on it in faith that Sammy was okay, when she really wasn't.

However, when I finally was able to have a baby shower for Hosanna, the quilt surprisingly made its appearance in my life once again. The finished project was given as a gift from our church secretary, Barbara, who had been tasked by my mom to finish it. This quilt was hard even for Barbara to finish because the type of material my friend and I had chosen was fragile and hard to work with. So, she needed to acquire other material to finish it. It was absolutely beautiful. It's not something that can be used as a regular blanket because of its fragility, but unwrapping it was incredibly overwhelming in the best way possible.

The quilt seemed to represent the community that had come out to support me in my journey to motherhood. It started alone, unfinished, broken, and fragile. Then, with the help of others, it started coming together as pieces were added to provide stability and support. The pieces were from many parts of the world, which seemed fitting as I had received support from the friends who had become family from all around the world. Lastly, though, it cannot be used as a quilt to keep my kids warm, it hangs in the kids' room as a reminder that God pieces together what is broken until it is finished with a purpose.

> "Yet, God has made everything beautiful for its own time. He has planted eternity in the human heart, but even so, people cannot see the whole scope of God's work from beginning to end."
>
> (Ecclesiastes 3:11 NLT)

21

How Others Can Help

The journey that I have shared took much longer to write than my first book because it was even more raw and heart-wrenching. There were many highs and lows, and I know that if Jesus did not place such incredible people in my life to support me, I would not have experienced the healing to the depth that I had, and I hope the same was done for you.

If you are reading simply to understand what someone is enduring, thank you. I hope you have discovered some practical ways to support your friend. The list below is not exhaustive, but important to consider:

1. Listen. When my friends traveled the four hours from Phoenix to simply ask me to tell them what I wanted to share, I knew I wasn't alone. They wanted to know my perspective so they

could be there for me the way I needed. Don't listen *just* to give advice. Offer an ear and a shoulder. Once your friend has finished sharing, ask how you can show him/her love. Don't assume anything.

2. Validate. Please don't EVER share that you think your friend should "get over it." This grief is so unique and isolating, there isn't even a word for someone who has lost his/her baby. There are widows, widowers, orphans, but the only thing for a parent is "bereaved parent" which, in many people's minds, has an expiration date. Don't be part of that problem. Know that many of the readers who appear to have moved on likely pushed down some of the pain in order to feel like they can function. My parents were a perfect example that there is healing left even twenty years later.
3. Be okay with grief. This goes in tandem with number two, but don't be so uncomfortable that you simply just say some of the common platitudes to "help someone feel better." Those platitudes rarely help, and if you look at their origin, they are quite self-centered attempts to stop the discomfort one feels when seeing another grieving. Before speaking, ask yourself, "Does this show my support and love? How would I feel hearing this? Would I tell this to someone who lost their dad or husband?" If the answer is "No" to any of these questions, keep it to yourself.
4. Offer support in closure. Maybe your friend wants to write a letter, celebrate birthdays, release something, make a craft, etc. to celebrate their little one. Do it with them. Help them gather the materials. Let them know it is important to you too. In most cases that I have seen, closure is almost always up to the parent. And in that state of grief, having a friend offer to help could be a breath of fresh air. Lisbet and Juvy prove a perfect example of how meaningful it is to have someone show up. This goes for churches too. If we want to continue the narrative that life begins at conception, then the loss of that life should be honored and acknowledged no matter how young. Very few churches I

know of offer any type of memorial. Be one that does. It will make a *huge* difference. Be like the church in the Philippines who went out of their way to acknowledge me as a mommy too.

5. Remember the important days, and if your friend does something to honor their baby, offer to take part. When it was Sammy's first Heavenly birthday, I had posted about how we were going to honor her, and I received so many private messages of encouragement, and pictures of friends lighting a candle, or eating a cupcake in her honor. It was the most heart-warming thing that I continue to treasure so deeply. That simple action showed me that again, I was supported and cared for.

> "Since God chose you to be the holy people he loves, you must clothe yourselves with tenderhearted mercy, kindness, humility, gentleness, and patience."
>
> (Colossians 3:12 NLT)

22

A Renewed Vision, a Song, & a Prayer

When I recall the vision of Heaven that I felt the Lord gave me when I had lost Sammy, I now see my little Micah. He and Sammy are both the most free-spirited little children, loving to run through the fields of flowers in Heaven, laughing and playing with Jesus. I so desperately desire still to see their features, to hear their laughter, but for now, I am at peace that I will one day be reunited with them. For now, I must be the best mama in the world to my sweet little blessings on Earth, telling them about the hope Jesus gives, and teaching them how to praise Him forever with their lives. For now, their mommy and daddy need to be there for the other mommies and daddies with babies in Heaven.

***

Chris

To Our Children,

(Chorus)

I can hear the tender whisper of my children's hearts.
How can we feel so close even though we are apart?
I hope you can feel my love as I yell it to the wind.
I hope you're there to meet me when my eternity begins.

(Verse)

My dear little babies, I hope that you can hear me.
Right now, as I write this, I'm staring at your mommy.
My Father thought it best that you stay with Him still.
I'm sorry we didn't get to meet, but one day I know we will.
Your mother longs to hold you, Father please send her a sign.
Help her in this time to truly understand why.
We don't understand everything that you have planned.
When she's crying out in pain, please send the Spirit to hold her hand.
I hope from your room in Heaven that you can see your mommy.
In the visions that I've seen of you, I swear you look just like her.
Right now, Lord, all I want is for my wife to see them too.
But even though this hurts, give us hearts to worship you.

(Chorus)

(Verse 2)

We'll hold you in our hearts until we can hold you in heaven.
What will you think of me? I can't even imagine.
It kills me to think I have children I didn't get to know.
And now I have you marked inside my skin; I'm not letting go.
Tell me, is it as great there as we've all been told?
Do the angels play with you? Are the streets made of gold?
Do you chase the warmth of God's light? Does He hold you if you're cold?

Does the rest of our family know you're there? I hope that they were told.
That you were coming, and they met you at the gates.
When I walk through the gates myself, will you recognize my face?
Will you ever feel the love I kept for you over the years?
Please don't feel sad for us, you're worth all these tears.

***

Denelle

As I end, I want to end in a prayer for you. We have begun a very difficult and painful journey that I can only hope has led to further healing, and a desire for a deeper relationship with the ultimate Healer. I encourage you to continue on this journey, even after the pages are closed.

Jesus, please be with the readers of this book, and their families. Some wounds are still so fresh, while others have been bandaged long ago in an attempt to stop the pain. Lord, please affirm the readers of their purpose, and the hope that only You give. I pray for complete healing over wombs, hearts, minds, and souls. For those whose hearts have been hardened, soften them. Show the readers the darkest areas of their hearts that need healing. Rescue the readers from envy, jealousy, bitterness, depression, anxiety, and other negative emotions that threaten to overtake them. Give them a glimpse of the rainbow of hope that you have set before them, whether in healthy babies, or some other blessing. Be with the readers; guide them, lead them, give them peace and joy. Speak truth to their hearts and meet them where they are in their healing journey. You started a work within them, and I pray that you continue your work until it is finally finished on the day when you return.

In Jesus' precious name I pray; amen.

"He heals the brokenhearted and bandages up their wounds."

(Psalms 147:3 NLT)

"And I am certain that God, who began the good work within you, will continue his work until it is finally finished on the day when Christ Jesus returns."

(Philippians 1:6 NLT)

Your turn: In your final response, write out some of your next steps in your journey through healing.

Other reflections or prayers:

Other Resources

Burpo, Todd. *Heaven is For Real.*

Greaux, Erin. *Inconceivable Redemption: God's Presence in Miscarriage & Infertility.*

Hayford, Jack. *I'll Hold You in Heaven.*

Philpott PHD, Sarah. *Loved Baby.*

For a sharing your story with a living child: Vis, Leah. *Our Heaven Baby.*

If you do not have a relationship with Jesus but have experienced that little stirring in your heart to learn more, please visit a local church, reach out to Denelle or Chris, or go to: https://peacewithgod.net and be paired with someone who will meet you where you are.

Other Works by the Authors:

Denelle Scanlan- *Sex in Marriage: From a Four-Letter Word to a Holy Act*

What happens when a young woman marries who has been told "having sex is sin"?

Denelle Scanlan struggled with feelings of shame, guilt, and fear as she transitioned from keeping herself pure to having a healthy sexual relationship with her husband. The incomplete message of the Christian purity culture can cause shame, guilt and fear when young women constantly hear negatives about sex, but are not told the positives of sexual intimacy in marriage. This candid personal narrative of a young woman coming to terms with sexual intimacy in marriage after growing up hearing only negatives includes her husband's viewpoint, journal prompts, and biblical truth.

Follow along in Denelle's journey of discovering: God designed sexual intimacy in marriage as a beautiful form of worship. God cares deeply about our healing there is hope beyond shame. How the church needs to address sex as a positive addition to marriage. *Sex in Marriage: From a Four-Letter Word to a Holy Act* is a way to get a conversation about sexual intimacy within marriage out in the open.

Chris Scanlan- *The Rainsbarger Brothers*

Murder, counterfeiting, lynch mobs, and shootouts! What do they all have to do with a band of brothers called the Rainsbargers?

In the 1880's, this small town family would become the famous name that it is today. Caught in the crossfire of two warring classes of people, the Rainsbargers would soon become known as infamous outlaws, destined for vigilante justice.

Enoch "Horsethief" Johnson's death caused an uproar within the small communities of Steamboat Rock and Elora, Iowa. Was it murder, or an accident, and what was the brothers' involvement?

"Help! Help! Murder! People of Eldora! For god's sake, help!"

Printed in the USA
CPSIA information can be obtained
at www.ICGtesting.com
LVHW090353300524
781287LV00007B/714

9 798218 415532